THE BOOK OF CACTI AND OTHER SUCCULENTS

THIS BOOK COURTESY OF
THE PUBLIC ENRICHMENT FOUNDATION AND
THE ALPENA-MONTMORENCY-ALCONA
INTERMEDIATE SCHOOL DISTRICT

THE BOOK OF CACTI AND OTHER SUCCULENTS

by CLAUDE CHIDAMIAN

Drawings by Shirlea Hatcher

TIMBER PRESS
Portland, Oregon
1984

Copyright © 1958 by Claude Chidamian
Designed by Joseph P. Ascherl
All rights reserved
Printed in the United States of America
ISBN 0-917304-90-X

Reprint edition, 1984, by
TIMBER PRESS
P.O. Box 1631
Beaverton, Oregon 97075

For LOIS

Contents

LIST OF ILLUSTRATIONS   ix

ACKNOWLEDGMENTS   xi

ONE *Introducing Succulents*   1

What Are Succulents?—How Succulents Developed—Dry Plants and Succulents—Where Succulents Grow—The Patterns of Survival

TWO *Understanding Succulents*   17

The Lure of Succulents—Five Famous Fallacies—A Problem and a Paradox—An Embarrassment of Riches

THREE *The Cactus Family*   25

What Are Cacti?—History and Nomenclature—The Leafy Cacti—The Prickly Pears and Chollas—The Cereus Tribe—The Torch Cacti—The Climbing Cacti—The Hedgehog Cacti—The Living Rock, Barrel, Star, Chin, and Ball Cacti—The Melon Cacti—The Pincushion Cacti—The Tree-dwelling Cacti

FOUR *Other Succulent Families* 63

The Amaryllis Family—The Crassula Family—The Daisy Family—The Euphorbia Family—The Lily Family—The Mesembryanthemum Family—The Milkweed Family—Succulents in Other Families

FIVE *Succulents in the Home* 133

Succulents as House Plants—Containers and Potting—Dish Gardens—Arrangements—Corsages

SIX *Succulents in the Garden* 159

The Rock Garden—Patterned Bedding—Wall and Ground-Cover Plantings—Espaliers, Planters, and Baskets

SEVEN *Collecting, Buying, and Propagating* 185

Collecting—Buying—Propagating

EIGHT *Maintenance* 203

Water—Rest—Cold and Shelter—Air, Light, and Shade—Food—Pruning and Weeding—Labels and Cataloguing

NINE *Pests and Diseases* 215

Sucking Pests—Chewing Pests—Fungus Diseases—Physiological Disturbances—The Human Element

TEN *Books About Succulents* 227

INDEX 231

List of Illustrations

Drawings

- 5 How the Wastelands Were Formed
- 11 How Succulents Developed
- 31 The Leafy Cacti, Prickly Pears, and Chollas
- 37 The Torch and Climbing Cacti
- 45 The Hedgehog Cacti
- 49 The Living Rock, Barrel, Star, Chin, and Ball Cacti
- 53 The Melon and Pincushion Cacti
- 59 The Tree-dwelling Cacti
- 65 The Amaryllis and Daisy Families
- 71 The Crassula Family
- 79 The Crassula Family
- 89 The Euphorbia Family
- 99 The Lily Family
- 111 The Mesembryanthemum Family
- 123 The Milkweed Family
- 129 Other Succulent Families
- 141 How to Pot Succulents
- 161 How to Plant Succulents
- 191 How to Grow Succulents from Seed
- 195 How to Make Cuttings and Divisions
- 199 How to Graft
- 219 Pests and Diseases

Photographs

- 21 As dramatic-accent plants in the home or garden succulents are unsurpassed.

137 A sunny window, two glass shelves, and a remarkable collection prove better than words that succulents can be easy and exciting house plants.

145 What could be simpler—or more beautiful—than a brass kettle planted with the purple rosettes of *Aeonium arboreum* var. *atropurpureum?*

147 Any patio or porch will become the center of attraction when decorated with a few succulents.

151 Aeonium blooms and rosettes form a striking arrangement.

155 A beautiful and lasting holiday arrangement is created with a few soft red- and silver-tinted rosettes of echeveria and graptopetalum.

165 The succulent bed should always be gently sloped and shaped in an interesting free-form pattern.

167 A few large rocks, carefully placed, enhance any succulent planting.

171 This spectacular mass planting of cacti displays dozens of *Echinocactus grusonii* blooming in the foreground and three clusters of tall columnar cacti in the center.

175 More and more, succulents are leaving the rock garden and desert planting to move into the perennial border and informal flower bed.

177 Succulents are perfect plants for banks and ground covers, terraces and rock walls.

181 Many succulents make beautiful and easy-to-care-for hanging-basket plants.

209 Good lighting, ventilation, and cleanliness are the secrets of successful succulent culture under glass.

223 Many collectors are fascinated by the relatively common occurrence of deformed or fasciated growths in succulents.

Acknowledgments

For their help in preparation of this book I would like to thank the following:

The editors of *Sunset* for permission to paraphrase briefly two of my articles on succulents originally published in their magazine. Scott E. Haselton, Editor Emeritus of the *Cactus and Succulent Journal*, for the photographs by J. R. Brown of the Ganna Walska collection on pages 21, 145, 147, 171, 177, 181; and for the photographs on pages 137, 165, 167, 209, and 223 (by Ladislaus Cutak). Nell True Welch for the photographs of her garden and succulent arrangements on pages 151, 155 (by William C. Eymann), and 175, used here by permission of Iva Newman, Garden Editor, San Mateo *Times*. And, certainly, Shirlea Hatcher, who captured in her drawings for this book not only the botanical details but the very heart and spirit of these exciting and intricate plants.

Finally, I would like to thank Robert Foster of Abbey Garden Press for help in preparing the revised bibliography of this edition, and Charles Glass, Editor of the *Cactus and Succulent Journal*, for the color photograph on the cover.

CLAUDE CHIDAMIAN

Laguna Beach, California,
February, 1984

THE BOOK OF CACTI AND OTHER SUCCULENTS

CHAPTER ONE

Introducing Succulents

Dramatic, exciting, always interesting—succulents have moved in and out of American homes and gardens on changing tides of popularity. While some collectors have remained loyal over the years, others have turned to succulents twice with serious interest—once in the nineties and again in the late twenties, when the succulent-cactus planting was part and parcel of the Spanish-style home.

Now succulents are coming back into favor again, but this time it is something more than a temporary infatuation. Modern gardeners have found in succulents landscape specimens that blend perfectly with contemporary architecture, house plants that require practically no care, ground covers that are as easy as they are beautiful, and flowers that put the choicest orchids to shame. Today succulents are earning their way by performance. They are no longer prized as oddities, but as the most elegant and practical plants it is possible to grow in our homes and gardens.

But despite this rising popularity, despite the dozens of books, hundreds of articles, and thousands of catalogues published on succulents in recent years, the beginner is still too often at a loss to know how and where to begin with these wonderful plants.

Certainly this simple book is not meant to replace the great monographs on cacti and other succulents, the lavishly illustrated picture books, or the serious surveys and descriptive lists. Many of these works are cited in the bibliography, and the reader is urged to study them carefully if he would go further with this great group of plants. But what this volume hopes to do is something none of these books has ever quite accomplished: to give the beginner a simple perspective, a coherent introduction to this most fascinating and complex group of plants in the whole world.

What Are Succulents?

A little cactus blooming bravely in a tenement window, a cluster of "Hen and Chickens" in an old garden, the lofty spire of a Century Plant, the dark candelabra of a giant Saguaro silhouetted against a brazen desert sky—these are succulents. They get their name from the Latin *succulentus,* which means juicy or fleshy, because they are all drought-resistant plants especially adapted to taking up and storing great quantities of water in their thick leaves, stems, or branches.

The succulents do not belong to any one family of plants. There are one or more succulent species in nearly thirty plant families. Although the cacti are perhaps the best-known family of succulents, it is important to remember that all succulents are not cacti. There are succulent plants in the Lily and Amaryllis families, the Daisy and Milkweed clan—even the Geranium family. Scores of common plants in our homes and gardens have curious succulent relatives the world over. But the story of succulents is not told with a simple definition.

How Succulents Developed

The story of succulents begins nearly fifty million years ago in a time called the Eocene epoch. A great waterway stretched from the Gulf of Mexico to the Arctic then. The Mediterranean lay deep in Asia. A hundred nameless seas covered our great deserts and mountains. Along their shores vast forests teemed with the beginnings of modern plants and animals. Everywhere the climate was subtropical, moist, abundant. Life was easy.

Then gradually the earth began to change. The ancient seas slowly retreated, revealing great new masses of land. Deep tremors shook the fields and forests, thrusting up great mountain barriers: the Rockies, the Sierra Nevadas, the Cascades— the Alps, Carpathians, and Pyrenees. A hundred volcanos formed the Andes. A new world began to take shape, a different world, the modern world we know today.

As the face of the earth changed, so did its climate. The year-round warmth and rains of the Eocene jungle gradually disappeared. In their place clearly marked seasons and climatic belts developed. There was a spring and summer now, a fall and winter. There were the Arctic and Antarctic, the tropics and Temperate Zone. Where there had been nothing but endless steaming jungle over much of the world, there were now high mountains, fertile plains, and endless deserts.

As the mountains rose in many parts of the world they gradually cut off the moisture-laden air blowing in from the seacoasts. And where the rain clouds could no longer cross the mountain barriers, the lands beyond the ranges burned by day and froze by night. What little rain they got reached them by winds coming from other routes, or in brief summer thundershowers formed out of the hot air rising from the desert floor.

At this time, too, a permanent belt of high atmospheric pressure developed extending some thirty or thirty-five degrees on each side of the equator. In this belt erratic winds and frequent calms prevented much rain from forming or falling. And from this lack of rain the world of the desert evolved—a very special world, with its own geography and climate, its own plants and animals, its own rhythm and way of life. In this way the Great Basin of North America was formed; the deserts of Mexico, Peru, Chile, and Argentina; the vast hinterlands of Asia and Africa. Gradually, very gradually, much of the Eocene world became a wasteland.

As wind and water eroded the rising mountains, the valleys below filled deep with earth and rock. The deserts stretched from mountainous plateaus to flat sandy plains. Where the wind was strong, the moving sand carved fantastic shapes in the rocks or piled high in rolling dunes. Where it sometimes rained, the water dissolved the mineral-rich earth, leaving behind great salt lakes.

Then new rivers rising beyond the desert entered the drying land just as it was lifting from its ancient bed. Filled with sand and rock, the grinding torrents cut through the earth, forming deep canyons, for there was no rain here to wash over the cuts—to widen them gently into broad river valleys. The sheer canyon cliffs, the great salt lakes, the dunes, the cactus—drought made them all.

Before the drought came, the Eocene fields and forests abounded with plants—remarkably modern plants, complete with roots, stems, leaves, flowers, and seeds. They were of many different families, forerunners of our lilies and oaks, gourds and palms. In the warm, moist climate they grew rampant.

Then came the change. It did not happen in a day or a year: it happened gradually. Some say it took twenty million years.

At first the year-round warmth and rains were interrupted for only a little while. The plants in the fields and forests took it in their stride, just as they would in our gardens today. They slowed their growth, branches shriveled a little, a few leaves wilted and fell. Soon the "bad spell" was over and they flourished again as strong as ever. But when the waters began receding in the ancient lakes and seas, when the rising hills became great ranges shutting off moisture from the coast—

INTRODUCING SUCCULENTS

HOW THE WASTELANDS WERE FORMED

the dwindling plants struggled desperately for life, tried to live out a few more weeks of drought, then a few months, then a year. Before the rains came again, most of them died.

Only a few survived. By some miracle they kept pace with the drying land, changed themselves endlessly, waited patiently, and in the end inherited the wastelands of the world. As a group these plants are called xerophytes (ze'-ro-fites), from the Greek words meaning "dry plants." They include not only such curiously adapted desert dwellers as the yucca, ocotillo, palo verde, mesquite, and sagebrush; but that remarkable group of plants we call succulents.

Dry Plants and Succulents

We do not know whether these xerophytes remained in the drying land throughout the whole process of their evolution, changing and adapting themselves to become desert dwellers over a period of twenty million years, or whether the wastelands became extinct of all life and these plants were hardy pioneers who ventured gradually into the barren lands from more favorable surrounding areas. But we do know they managed to survive the scant rainfall, the long periods of drought, the intense heat and cold of the wastelands by using one or more of these three devices: economizing, lying low, and storing.

First, all xerophytes learned to economize. The broad, lush leaves of the Eocene jungle which transpired untold gallons of water into the air each day were reduced in size; were covered with wax, resin, or hair; or rolled until they became almost like needles. The stomata, or leaf pores, were reduced in number. Stems and branches often became thin, hard, and dry. The sap became thick, sticky, or milky. All this was done to save precious moisture—to prevent quick evaporation, wilting, and death.

Then some xerophytes learned to lie low. They clung to the

shadow of rocks and such vegetation as there was. They buried themselves in the long months of drought and became seemingly as dead and dry as dormant seeds.

And, finally, some learned to store—to come to life quickly at the first sign of a shower, to greedily drink with widespreading roots even the lightest dew. And to store this precious moisture some developed great tuberous roots, and others thick, fleshy leaves, stems, and branches. It is these last—xerophytes which learned to store water in greatly enlarged leaves, stems, and branches—that we call "succulents."

It is very difficult to draw a sharp line of distinction between succulents and other xerophytes, or xerophytes and ordinary plants. In many plant families we can find a wide range of drought resistance—from soft, lush, tropical plants requiring an abundance of moisture through every degree of drought resistance until we reach true succulents. Thus in the Lily family we have the tropical Bermuda or Easter lily, the relatively drought-resistant asparagus, the xerophytic yucca and its relatives of our Southwest, and the truly succulent aloes of South Africa—and every conceivable gradation in between.

We do not know why plants belonging to the same family became simple xerophytes in one place, as the yuccas in our Southwest, and succulent in another, as the aloes in South Africa. The tendency toward succulence seems to have been inherent in certain members of a family and not in others. Then, too, the peculiar conditions of geography, climate, and development no doubt determined the type of response each plant was to make.

Actually succulence in plants—the ability to store water—is a relative thing. All plants store some water in their roots, stems, and leaves to meet days and weeks of hardship. Some even show exceptional ability to store moisture in bulbs, rhizomes, and tubers to withstand months of dormancy. But in the succulents this ability to store moisture against even years of drought is so highly developed as to be unique. While other xerophytes evolved thinner, harder, drier stems and leaves to resist the endless heat and thirst of the wastelands, the succulents made these parts larger, thicker, fleshier to serve as storage spaces for water. It is no wonder they have been called "camels of the plant world."

Where Succulents Grow

Succulents are found almost anywhere in the world today where plants have difficulty getting and keeping water. Specifically there are four geographical areas that are the natural habitat of succulents. They might be termed the desert, alpine, jungle, and shore line.

The first and most important of these are the great deserts and semi-arid brushlands of North and South America, Africa, and Asia. Here intense heat, sandy soil, lack of rainfall, and drying winds have given rise to the largest natural habitat of succulents. But it is important to know that not all the deserts of the world have native succulent plants. Extreme deserts such as the Sahara, Gobi, and Great Sandy Plain of Australia afford so little moisture that few if any succulents have been able to grow in them. Here we find only xerophytic thornbushes and low annuals growing in the shifting dunes. Other desert areas often lack succulent plants too, because these wastelands have been formed too quickly to allow for the gradual evolution required to develop succulents, or the xerophytic plants in the area have had no inherent tendency toward succulence. But in all other desert areas where rainfall exceeds a very few inches annually and climatic conditions are not too extreme we can expect to find succulent plants.

Strangely enough, succulents are also found in the tropical rain forests of Central and South America, where, although rainfall is abundant, certain tree-dwelling cacti have developed succulence because they get scant moisture from the

INTRODUCING SUCCULENTS

bits of moss and bark in which they are rooted high in the trees.

Another important area where succulents may be found is the high mountain regions of the world. Here many plants have become succulent because intense cold, strong winds, and a loose, rocky soil have made getting and keeping water difficult.

And, finally, succulents are found on the shores of salt lakes and seas, where the brackish ground makes the absorption of water difficult for plants. In all these places the struggle over millions of years for life-giving moisture has changed many familiar plants into highly specialized succulent forms.

The Patterns of Survival

Despite their amazing variety and number all succulents may be classified in one or another of two groups—leaf succulents or stem succulents. Plants belonging to the class known as monocotyledons, such as the lilies, usually took on the form known as leaf succulence. The leaves of these plants were greatly thickened and crowded into a cluster or rosette, either with or without a fleshy or woody stem. Plants belonging to the class known as dicotyledons, such as the cacti, took in addition still another form. With them the stem was greatly enlarged to serve as a storehouse for water and to carry on the vital functions of photosynthesis, and the leaves were either much reduced and short-lived or dropped altogether.

But much more important than the outward changes and forms these plants took are the immense internal changes they had to undergo before they could become succulents. Their main problem was getting and keeping moisture more efficiently. And they solved it in a thousand ingenious ways.

First, they had to get water. Rainfall in the wastelands was seasonal and brief. The succulents had to drink thirstily and well for a few hours or days each year, and then wait months before they could slake their thirst again. To gather this precious moisture they developed a fantastic variety of root systems according to the soil and climate in which they lived.

Succulents living in areas of extreme drought often developed great tuber-like roots to store water between rains. Others in the rocky foothills and mountains sent their roots deep into the moist substrata underlying the surface. Others on the open plains developed a fine network of roots spreading for yards about the plant but only an inch or two beneath the surface in order to catch the lightest dew. Actually the roots of most succulents are so extensive and interlaced that if these plants were turned upside down the sparse and scrubby wastelands they inhabit would look like impenetrable jungles.

The next problem after the succulents soaked up their water was to keep it. They had to effectively prevent the excessive evaporation which the bright sun and drying wind of the desert could cause, for all plants in order to live must transpire a remarkable quantity of water through the pores in their leaves and stems. When we consider that a grass transpires its own weight in water daily, a stalk of corn more than a gallon a day, and an apple tree two thousand gallons in a single growing season—we can see the vital importance of curtailing this evaporation in succulents. When a succulent plant receives as its whole yearly supply as much water as a lush jungle plant expends in a single day, it obviously must hoard this precious moisture or die.

Like other xerophytes, the first and most obvious thing the succulents did was to economize. They shortened their leaves and stems, took on a more compact form to present less evaporating surface to the drying sun and wind. In the leaf succulents the plants grouped their leaves in tight clusters, one leaf overlapping another like shingles on a roof, protecting each other from the drying elements. The stem succulents reduced their leaves, rolling them into needle-like projections; or kept them only briefly during the short growing season

INTRODUCING SUCCULENTS

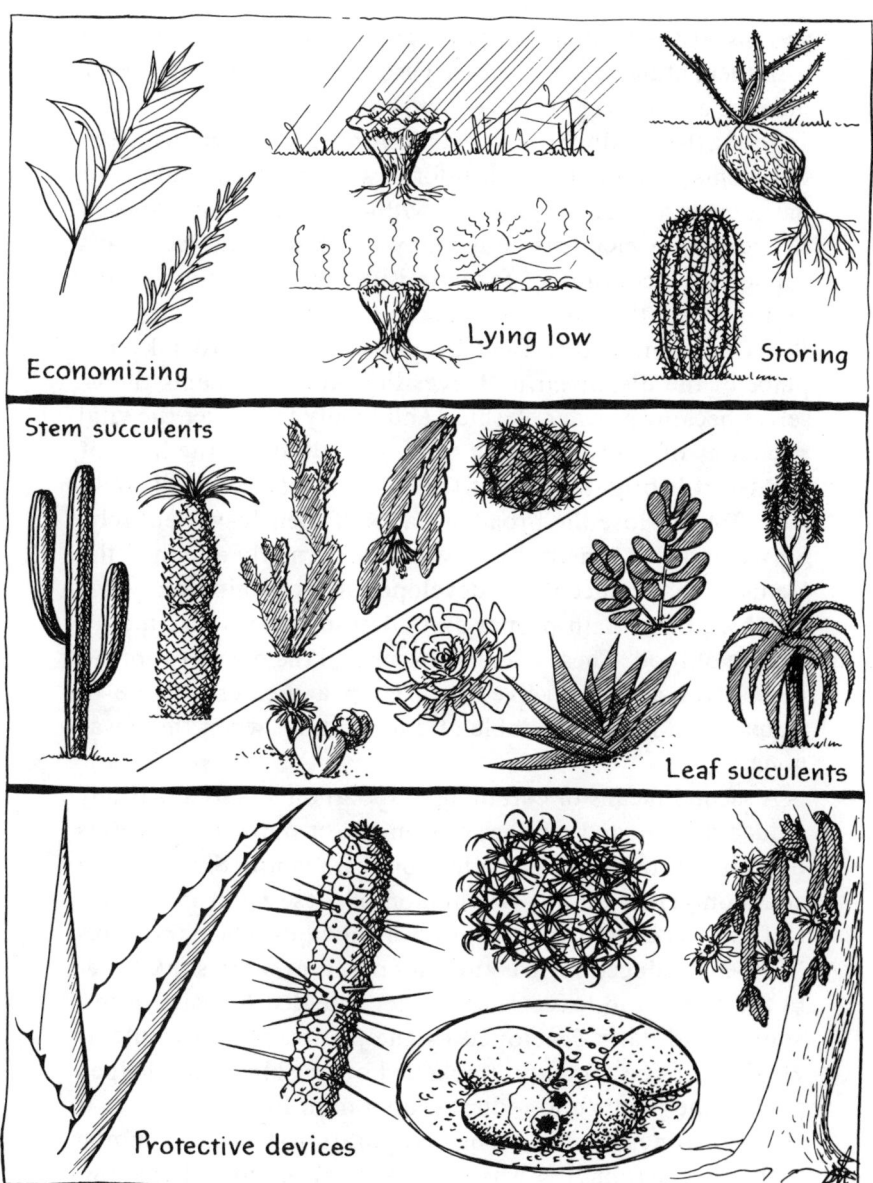

HOW SUCCULENTS DEVELOPED

and discarded them at the first sign of drought; or dispensed with them altogether to become perfect stem succulents, never showing a leaf except in the embryo stage.

To further reduce their evaporating surface many stem succulents took on a spherical form, a form which could hold the greatest amount of moisture with the least surface exposed to the drying elements. But many of these stem succulents carried the economy of form and loss of leaves too far, for they needed the green assimilating surfaces of leaves and stems to manufacture food by photosynthesis. To take the place of the disappearing leaves the succulent stems themselves became greener, fleshier, and finally took over the vital processes of manufacturing food. But although the light of the desert is bright, many of these stem succulents still could not afford to lose the broad surfaces of their leaves entirely. So we find that where the leaves were formerly attached the stems of many succulents developed nobs or nipples, wings or ribs, to maintain proper assimilation of light and manufacture of food. These ribs also permitted the plants to spread themselves accordion-like to take up a greater volume of water when it was available and to contract when there was none.

A second means of curtailing evaporation was to drastically reduce the size and number of stomata, or pores, in the leaves or stems through which water could transpire. Since even a common geranium has two million of these pores in a single leaf, the necessity for reduction was obvious. Once the pores had been reduced in size and number, they were sunk lower in the stems and leaves and further shielded by wax, resins, spines, and hairs developed by the plants. Most succulents also developed a greatly thickened outer skin which helped protect the plants and reduce evaporation further.

A third means of reducing evaporation, held in common with other xerophytes, was the clever expedient of lying low. Many succulents learned to bury themselves almost entirely in the soil, to expose as little of themselves as possible to the outside world. Others learned to cling desperately to the shade of rocks and other desert plants.

But as the supply of water the succulents could take up in any rainy season was small, and that which they gave off in the long periods of drought even less, the whole internal chemistry of succulents changed. Since plants can absorb food from the soil only when it is dissolved in water, and since the intake of water in succulents was never very great, the assimilation of food was slowed down tremendously. This explains why succulents are relatively slow-growing, slow-living plants.

And as the chemical processes in the plants slowed up, there appeared a greater tendency toward the accumulation of by-products. Some of these were seemingly useless to the plant, as calcium oxalate, which crystallizes in enormous quantities in the cells of some cacti. Other by-products, such as wax, deposited on the outer skin served the useful purpose of reducing evaporation and partially shielding the pores. It is even possible that the elaborate formation of stiff hairs, bristles, and spines in desert plants is actually the result of too great accumulations of silicon, an element useless for nourishment but giving rigidity to plant parts. This silicon, concentrated in modified leaf stalks, branches, and flower stems, produces the characteristic armament of many succulents. Certainly these teeth and spines not only serve to protect the plants from browsing animals, but often form a latticework to shade the body of the plant and further reduce evaporation.

Once they had adapted themselves to getting and keeping water, the succulents had to make further changes to protect themselves. Since they were the best source of food and moisture for herbivorous animals in the wasteland, they had to protect themselves or be eaten. Some, like the cacti, agaves, and aloes, armed themselves with sharp spines or teeth. These weapons were always on the most projecting parts of the stems or leaves, and the tender heart of the plant was usually sunk deep inside their protective cover. Others, lacking this armament, developed a strong, thick skin, like many of the gasterias. Some, like the sedums and epiphyllums, grew in rocks or trees out of reach. Others, such as the lithops, camouflaged themselves, mimicking the texture and color of their surroundings so that they could not be seen. Still others, like the windowed plants, buried themselves in the soil almost entirely, admitting light to their interiors through exposed "windows" in their leaf tips. And, finally, some protected themselves with repulsive or poisonous juices, as the quinine-flavored dudleya.

To further insure their survival in the wilderness nature designed succulents so that they could not only propagate themselves by seed, but also, in many species, multiply themselves spontaneously by fallen leaves, branches, or shoots. Wind, rain, or a blow from anything that passed could easily scatter the fleshy leaves and shoots, and because they carried their own moisture they could quickly root on dry ground. Other succulents, like the bryophyllums, formed tiny well-developed plants on their flower stems or leaves which fell to earth ready to grow. Even the green fruit of certain cacti can make a plant if they touch the soil. Of all plants the succulents are perhaps most efficiently designed by nature for easy propagation.

In a thousand different ways the succulents adapted themselves to a thousand different environments. But it was by no means a conscious adaptation. They did not perform any of these miracles deliberately. The process was the long and cruel selection of nature, in which only the fittest survived. And all these forms that remain today are simply the more successful experiments in that endless process of trial and error we call evolution.

Though they came from many different families, with different forms and habits, all these plants under the same pressures of necessity made similar changes in form, and in the end came to resemble each other. Before they could exist in the harsh climate of the wastelands, these lilies, amaryllids, daisies, and milkweeds had to adapt themselves to get and keep moisture more efficiently. Luckily they could adapt. For hidden in their stems and leaves was the quality of succulence, the ability to store more and more water to meet the ever lengthening seasons of drought. As millions of plants perished about them for lack of this gift, the succulents lived on. But in order to live they had to change endlessly. The broad leaves of the jungle grew smaller in each generation, grew thicker, or sometimes disappeared altogether. The rank jungle growth became shorter, heavier, changed in a thousand ways to conserve precious moisture. Each group of survivors, in its own way, in its own time, changed to meet the pressures of its own locality. Shaped by a hundred new climates, isolated by great mountain ranges, rooted in an endless variety of soils—the succulents took on the myriad forms we know today.

CHAPTER TWO

Understanding Succulents

In all the world no other plants are so wonderfully varied in form, so beautiful in flower, so remarkably adapted to life as the succulents. Yet none have been so thoroughly misunderstood.

How often we call any plant with an odd form or spines a cactus, no matter if it belongs to the Lily or Amaryllis family, the Daisy or Milkweed clan. How often we think of succulents as strange plants—half ugly, half comical—never to be compared with our pet roses and orchids, azaleas and camellias. And because of our blind prejudice we miss one of the most interesting and beautiful experiences the world of plants has to offer.

Understanding succulents is like understanding people. They seem odd and different until we learn something about them—where they came from, how they developed, how they were meant to live and grow. Then we begin to see beauty where there was only strangeness; we begin to feel a strong attraction where there was only fear and indifference before.

The Lure of Succulents

It is difficult for those who have not felt the lure of succulents to understand the powerful attractions they exert on those who love them. First, succulents offer variety to satisfy even the most insatiable gardener. They range in size from plants scarcely larger than a thimble to giants towering fifty feet high and weighing tons. Their forms are infinite.

But many gardeners are not interested in plant forms alone, they want flowers. Here too succulents will not be found wanting. Among them we can find the largest flowers on earth and some of the tiniest, blooms of such incredible textures and colors as to put our pampered orchids and camellias to shame. And the succulents offer color not only in their flowers, but in their stems and leaves, so often tinged with an iridescent bloom of frosty white, rich purple, or red. Even the feared teeth and spines intrigue us by their varied colors and intricate patterns.

But perhaps the thing that really seals the attraction between succulents and those who love them is the quiet lessons they teach of endurance and faith in life. How well they exemplify the virtues of patience and economy, the wisdom of lying low and rolling with the punches, of storing within ourselves those vital resources we will need in times of adversity. Succulents are strong plants, and they make those who grow them strong.

In our first chapter we have spoken of succulents becoming "adapted" to drought, of becoming "adjusted" to their environment. But we did not use those words in the sense in which sociologists so often use them today. Unlike people, succulents have not lost either their individuality or strength in meeting the demands of their environment. They have not simply made the *most* of life, as sociologists tell us we must, but the *best*. The difference is tremendous. These plants have met adversity and change with strength, not submission. They are not simply "adjusted" to their environment—they are triumphant in it.

UNDERSTANDING SUCCULENTS

Five Famous Fallacies

Before we can either see or appreciate the value of succulents, however, we must dispose of our basic fears and prejudices. There are perhaps no more persistent and ridiculous falsehoods in all the world of plants than these five famous fallacies concerning succulents.

1. *All succulents are cacti.* As we have seen, the Cactus family is only one of nearly thirty plant families which have succulent members. To be sure, it is one of the largest and best known—but it is not the only one. The beginner is perhaps understandably confused, because some succulents in other plant families sometimes resemble cacti very closely. But when one is in doubt, it is always safer to refer to these plants by the general term *succulents* rather than by the very specific family name *Cactus.*

2. *All succulents grow in the desert.* Although the deserts of the world contain the largest number and variety of succulents, not all succulents are desert dwellers. They are also found in tropical jungles, on high mountains, and by the shores of salt lakes and seas.

3. *All succulents grow in full, blazing sunlight.* The notion that succulents grow only in full sunlight is incorrect. Many succulents, even desert dwellers, prefer to grow in the partial shade of rocks and other plants rather than in the bright sun.

4. *All succulents grow in pure sand.* It is obvious from their wide variety of habitats that succulents grow in many different kinds of soil. Even the so-called pure sand of the deserts is far richer than one might suppose, as can readily be seen where portions of desert lands have been reclaimed for farming by irrigation.

5. *All succulents can live without water.* Although the succulents can probably grow with less water than any other

As dramatic-accent plants in the home or garden succulents are unsurpassed. *Agave attenuata* (ABOVE) and *Echeveria glauca* (BELOW) are combined here in a "strawberry jar" planter to make a striking study in gray.

group of plants, they must have a reasonable supply in order to continue life. This is clearly demonstrated by the fact that very extreme deserts, such as the Sahara, cannot support succulents simply because there is not enough rainfall.

A Problem and a Paradox

The fact that succulents are so well adapted to drought and hardship has led many gardeners to one or another of these false conclusions: that better care will necessarily improve the plants, or that lack of attention is the secret of successful succulent culture. Actually succulents often receive very particular care in nature, especially where soil and drainage are concerned, and too much kindness with water and fertilizers usually means sure death to them.

The problem in growing succulents is a strange one. Everything detrimental to them seems to be eliminated from our homes and gardens. They don't have to put up with dry soil, scorching sun, lack of water, or browsing animals. Yet there is a problem. Under cultivation these marvelously adapted plants often suffer. Their armor is useless; their compact form, juicy leaves, and thick skins are more a hindrance than a help. They are fitted with equipment they no longer need but cannot change. So it is up to the gardener to compensate for this paradox.

Success with succulents requires a good deal of observation, common sense and, above all, an understanding of where they came from and how they were meant to live and grow. But this is more easily said than done.

An Embarrassment of Riches

The collector of succulents is faced with an embarrassment of riches. In the Cactus family alone there are more than two thousand species, and the cacti are but one family in nearly thirty containing succulent plants. Fortunately of the tens of thousands of succulents known probably less than half have ever been cultivated by collectors. And of these, many, many hundreds are so rare, difficult to grow, unwieldy, or uninteresting that they are obviously useless to the beginner. But there still remain several thousand species and varieties from which we might choose. How can we decide which are the most beautiful, most interesting, most desirable to have in our collections?

Of course that question is not easily answered. For the selection of any plant depends on the needs and tastes, interests and purse of the individual gardener. But aside from that there are certain succulents that stand out from all the rest. They are the most popular, readily available, easily grown, and useful kinds in their respective families. They have stood the test of time and universal appeal. The beginner should know and grow these varieties first, and then move on to others as his skill and interest develop.

The chapters which follow attempt to suggest some of the "best" kinds in each family. But they are admittedly incomplete, not because the plants listed in them are not among the best, but because many who read them will wish to add a few more kinds in every family according to their individual tastes and experience. Of course that is to be encouraged, just as the hope that future years will see the arrival of many new succulent varieties that will eclipse some of these.

CHAPTER THREE

The Cactus Family

It is fitting that any discussion of succulents begin with the Cactus family, not only because it is one of the largest and best known but because it illustrates in a very surprising way the evolution of all succulent plants.

Were it not for a strange coincidence, we might never really know how succulents evolved from the Eocene jungles to their present way of life. Deserts, unlike marshes or lakes, are not very favorable to the preservation of fossil plants. So it is not surprising that the ancient forerunners of the succulents disappeared without a trace millions of years ago. But, as if to compensate for this lack of fossil evidence, nature has given us something infinitely more exciting. In the Cactus family today there is a remarkably complete set of *living* forms which illustrate step by step how this group of plants evolved from primitive, leafy jungle plants to highly specialized desert dwellers.

There exists in the jungles of the West Indies today a clambering tropical shrub or vine called a pereskia, which is, to an uncanny degree, the living image of the Eocene ancestor from which all our cacti evolved. And that is not all. We can also find in other living members of the Cactus family every gradation in the evolution of succulence from the lush, tropical pereskia to the most hard-bitten desert dweller. So instead of looking at fossil remains in a museum case we can actually see growing before our eyes the whole pattern of evolution in the Cactus family from Eocene jungle to modern desert succulents.

What Are Cacti?

The Cactus family is not clearly related to any other, though some have suggested a kinship with the portulacas, mesembryanthemums, myrtles, or even roses. It contains over two thousand species, virtually all of them full stem succulents. Although they differ widely in form, size, and habitat, all its members can be recognized by five common traits.

First, all cacti have a unique cushion-like structure on their stems and branches called an areole (a'-ree-ohl). Each areole has two growing points, or buds, the lower one generally producing spines and the upper one producing new branches or flowers. Second, cacti are perennial: that is, they require more than one season to mature, and they do not die after flowering. Third, cacti usually have wheel- or funnel-shaped flowers with an indefinite number of sepals and petals, and the ovary or fruit is always formed below the flower. Fourth, the cactus fruit is a one-celled berry with the seeds simply scattered through it. Fifth, all cacti belong to that class of flowering plants known as dicotyledons (dy-kot'-i-lee'-dun). Their seeds always produce two embryo leaves, or cotyledons, on germination. Any plant having all these traits is a cactus. If it lacks even one it is something else.

The Cactus family is native only to the American continent, ranging from the Arctic Circle to Patagonia. But its real home lies somewhere in the middle of that vast stretch, in the great American Southwest and northern Mexico. Here cacti are the outstanding feature of the great deserts and wastelands of California, Arizona, New Mexico, Texas, and Sonora.

THE CACTUS FAMILY

As one moves south, the number and variety of cacti decrease, until in tropical Central America and the Caribbean the desert species give way to curious tree-dwelling cacti. Below the tropics, in South America, the number of desert species rises again through Brazil, Bolivia, Paraguay, Uruguay, and Argentina, but never in such bewildering variety as in Mexico and the Southwest. Across the Andes, the deserts of Chile and Peru offer a large and unusual cactus population.

History and Nomenclature

Cacti were unknown in Europe before the discovery of America. When the early Spanish and Portuguese explorers landed in the New World they were amazed to find these strange plants, for they were not only a remarkable feature of the landscape, but were cultivated by the aborigines for food, timber, drugs, and drink.

It is not surprising that they took these plants, particularly the edible Prickly Pears, back with them first to the Canaries, Azores, and Madeira Islands; then Portugal, Spain, and the whole Mediterranean. From there the Prickly Pears spread to Egypt, India, and other parts of southern Asia, becoming an important food in many areas, a serious pest in some, and a remarkable curiosity in others.

The first cacti that reached Europe must indeed have seemed plants from another world. The date of their introduction is not known, though the explorer Coronado mentions them in his account of the New World in 1540. But in 1597 we find pictures and descriptions of two cacti in England. Gerarde in his book *The Herball or Generall Historie of Plantes* is completely astounded by the common Prickly Pear, which he calls Ficus Indica, or the prickly Indian Fig Tree. And of a second species, the Turk's Cap from the West Indies, he writes:

> Who can but maruell at the rare and singular Workmanship which the Lord God almightie hath shewed in this thistle, called

by the name *Echino-melocactus* or *Melo-carduus Echinatus*. This knobbie or bunchie masse or lumpe is strangely compact and context togither, containing in it sundry shapes or formes, participating of a Pepon or Melon, and a Thistle, both being incorporate in one bodie; which is made after the forme of a cocke of haie...

With such remarkable descriptions, it is not surprising that the number of cacti in Europe increased rapidly. But with them stuck the idea that they were somehow like thistles. When Linnaeus in 1753 listed twelve of these plants in his *Species Plantarum* he grouped them all under the name Cactus, derived from the Greek *kaktos,* which is the ancient name for a prickly thistle or cardoon. Thereafter this family of plants has been called the *Cactaceae* (kak-tay'-see-ee), single plants *cactus* (kak'-tus), more than one plant *cacti* (kak'-tie), rather than cactuses.

Through the eighteenth century and into the early part of the nineteenth interest in cacti grew tremendously as new plants were introduced to Europe. Gerarde's simple classification of Indian Figs and Melon-thistles and Linnaeus's grouping of the dozen plants he knew as "Cactus" could hardly begin to describe the scores of strange and varied plants that captivated European gardeners. Many botanists tried to put the ever growing list of cacti in some kind of order, but it remained for Karl Schumann to publish the first coherent classification of the family in his *Monograph on the Cactaceae* in 1898.

Schumann divided the Cactus family into three tribes in the probable order of their development: the Pereskia, the Opuntia, and the Cereus. But there were still far too many and varied cacti in each tribe for easy recognition, so Schumann divided the three tribes into twenty-one smaller groups called genera (the singular is genus). These genera, groups of plants in each tribe having certain obvious structural characteristics in common, contained in turn the thousands of individual kinds of cactus plants, or species. And these species in turn produced variants which are called varieties.

It may help to understand Schumann's plan, and the general method of scientific nomenclature, if we remember that the first part of a plant's scientific name is that of the genus to which it belongs; the second part, usually a qualifying adjective indicating *what kind,* is the species name; and, where necessary, a third part indicates the particular variety. Thus in the family *Cactaceae,* the tribe *Opuntieae,* we have the cactus *Opuntia fragilis* var. *tuberiformis. Opuntia* is the generic name of the plant; *fragilis* its specific name, indicating the Fragile Opuntia, a particular kind; and *tuberiformis,* the varietal name, which tells us that this variety of *Opuntia fragilis* has tuberlike stems.

Although Schumann's system was widely acclaimed and adopted in Europe, new botanical explorations in the Southwest, Mexico, and South America after the turn of the century brought to light hundreds of cacti that could not be explained by his classification. After extensive research and exploration under the auspices of the Carnegie Institute, Drs. N. L. Britton and J. N. Rose published a new and monumental American classification, *The Cactaceae,* in the years 1919 to 1923. Here they accepted Schumann's three tribes—the *Pereskieae,* the *Opuntieae,* and the *Cereeae*—but subdivided the last into eight subtribes, and the twenty-one genera into one hundred and twenty-four.

Since the publication of *The Cactaceae* new explorations have added many more cacti to the family, with suggestions for new classifications, subdivisions, and genera; but the basic work of Britton and Rose remains fundamentally sound and still the best guide to the vast and perplexing family of cacti. The brief survey of the Cactus family which follows is patterned somewhat after the Britton and Rose classification. But to simplify the recognition of cactus tribes and subtribes popular descriptive titles have been used suggesting the chief characteristics of each group, and only those genera and species of outstanding interest to the beginner are discussed.

CACTI AND OTHER SUCCULENTS

The Leafy Cacti—The *Pereskieae*

The first tribe of the Cactus family contains its most primitive members, for they are actually common jungle trees, shrubs, or vines. They may be easily differentiated from other cacti by their sprawling woody stems, ordinary broad evergreen leaves, and clusters of flat wheel-shaped flowers borne on stalks. Members of this tribe have two kinds of spines coming from their areoles: straight for protection, and hooked for climbing.

The genus *Pereskia* (per-es'-ki-ah) dominates this first tribe of the Cactus family. There are some eighteen or twenty species of pereskia native to the West Indies, Mexico, Central and South America. In the tropics they are grown as ornamentals or hedges, and the olive-sized yellow fruit of its most popular species are prized as "Barbados gooseberries."

Pereskia aculeata, commonly called the Lemon Vine, is that best-known species. It is a clambering, shrubby vine to ten feet or more with broad, flat leaves much the same shape, size, and color as a lemon leaf. The slender stems are first prickly, then develop long needle-like spines. Although sometimes difficult to bloom in cultivation, the clusters of fragrant, creamy-pink flowers are as charming as wild roses. A striking variety with leaves variegated red, apricot, yellow, and green on the upper side, and red purple on the underside, is called *P. aculeata* var. *godseffiana.*

For the collector pereskias are interesting as living examples of the kind of primitive non-succulent plants all cacti evolved from, and useful as understocks for grafting. Except in very favored localities the pereskias must be treated as tender plants for the home or greenhouse. They require rather large pots, abundant water in the growing season, and a minimum temperature above 50°F. They are easily propa-

THE CACTUS FAMILY

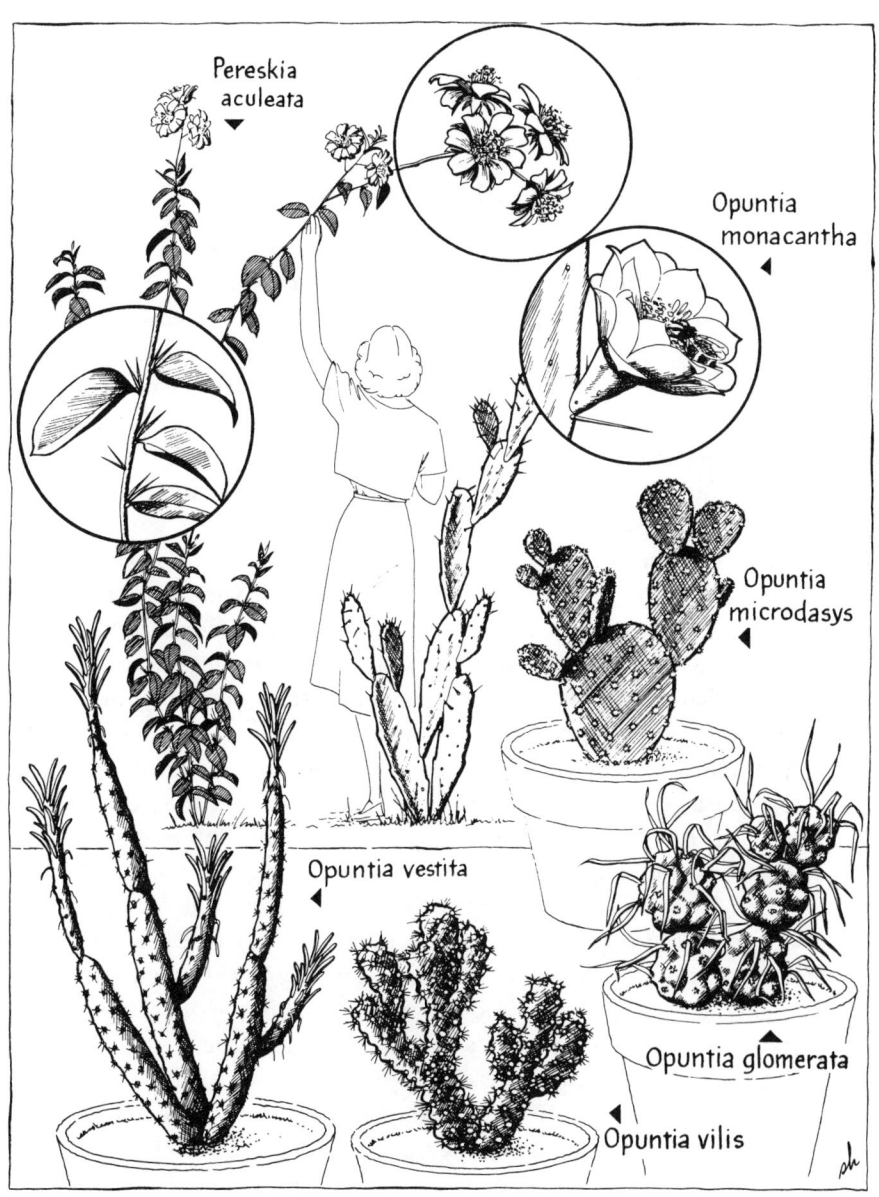

THE LEAFY CACTI, PRICKLY PEARS, AND CHOLLAS

gated by seed or cuttings, which, because of their broad leaves and limited succulence, should be rooted at once without the usual drying period.

The Prickly Pears and Chollas—The *Opuntieae*

Members of the second tribe of the Cactus family range from low shrubby plants to large treelike forms, sometimes with woody stems. But unlike the *Pereskieae,* they are full stem succulents with only small, cylindrical, transient leaves that usually fall off as the stem matures. Spines are usually present and always accompanied by tufts of characteristic barbed hairs called glochids (glo'-kid). The wide-open, wheel-shaped flowers are attached to the plant without a stalk and have a very short tube.

Of the nine genera in this tribe the one called *Opuntia* (oh-pun'-shi-ah) is the best known and most widely distributed. It is native to virtually all parts of the American continent from British Columbia to the southernmost tip of South America. Although it has more than three hundred species, showing a bewildering variety of forms and habits, they can be separated into three distinct groups according to the form of their stems or branches. First—the platyopuntias, or Prickly Pears—whose younger stems, at least, are flattened into pads or discs, one growing out of the other. Second—the tall cylindropuntias, or Chollas (cho'-yah)—whose cylindrical branches are joined together like sausages in long links. And third—the low-growing tephrocacti (tef-ro-kak'-tie)—with many short cylindrical or globe-shaped stems joined together only a link or two at a time.

Of all cacti the opuntias are probably the most important economically. Fruit of the Prickly Pears are highly prized in Mexico and along the Mediterranean, and the young stems are eaten as a green vegetable or used for cattle fodder. Before the advent of chemical dyes vast plantations of platyopuntias were maintained to feed the cochineal insect, which, when dried and powdered, produces a fine red dye still sometimes used in lipsticks.

As ornamental plants in landscaping the opuntias are more unusual than pleasing. Their stiff, formal appearance does not blend well with other plants, and their sharp spines and bristles can be a real hazard in the garden. But when planted en masse as hedges or in large natural groups where they can develop freely they make a striking show. Most species grow rapidly and bloom profusely with brilliant silky flowers, and the brightly colored fruit of some is wonderfully decorative. As house plants the opuntias are not quite so popular as they once were—probably because many species do not flower until the plants have grown quite large, because they take up a good deal of space, and because so many are wickedly armed. But by carefully selecting species suited to pot culture these problems can be eliminated.

Of the hundreds of species available the following are some of the most useful and interesting for the beginner. Among the platyopuntias *O. microdasys,* popularly called Bunny Ears, has long been a favorite house plant. This beautiful dwarf Mexican species has flat, oblong, spineless pads covered with bright golden tufts of soft glochids. It is available in a number of varieties with variously colored glochids ranging from white through yellow, red, and brown. An equally popular species is the Beaver Tail, *O. basilaris,* a low, spreading plant whose broad, spineless pads are actually shaped like beavers' tails and bear large purple flowers. Another curiously formed species is *O. erectoclada,* commonly called Dominoes. It is a dwarf, clustering plant whose flat trapeziform pads suggest free-form sculpture. The tall angular pads of *O. monacantha variegata,* strangely marked with green, white, and pink, have won for it the popular name Joseph's Coat. And perhaps the most striking of all the Prickly Pears is the Grizzly Bear Cactus, *O. erinacea,* which is prized for its thick hairy coat of white or yellowish-white spines. In the variety *ursina* these soft, flexible spines are sometimes a foot long.

Among the cylindropuntias there are three small species which have found great favor as house plants. The cylindrical branches of *O. mammillata* split into crests at the tips to resemble boxing gloves, hence its popular name. The branches of *O. vilis* make a small treelike growth for which it is given the name Mexican Dwarf Tree. It is wonderfully adapted to dish gardens, where it resembles a miniature Joshua tree. And the Old Man Opuntia, *O. vestita,* is a cylindrical Bolivian species beautifully covered with woolly white hair and striking awl-shaped leaves on its new growth.

Among the strange and sometimes difficult tephrocacti there are two very popular and relatively easy species. The spineless blue-gray *O. strobiliformis* looks for all the world like a pine cone. And the Paper-spined Opuntia, *O. glomerata,* is a short globular plant with fantastic papery spines sometimes four inches long. These spines are quite soft, flat, and thin, and seem as if made of old parchment. It is a "must" for every collection.

Because the opuntias are so numerous and varied, growing in a wide range of climates and soils, only the most general instructions can be given for growing them. Most species are of the easiest culture, preferring a rather poor sandy soil, a warm sunny location, and very moderate watering. Given too much shade or rich soil, especially indoors, the opuntias lose their character and grow rampant with long snaky branches. Properly grown, many species can take temperatures well below zero if kept dry.

Opuntias are very easy to grow from cuttings, and the green fruit of some species will form new plants if set in damp soil. Opuntia seeds are usually large and germinate easily, and seedlings or cuttings of the less spiny platyopuntias make excellent grafting stocks.

The Cereus Tribe—The *Cereeae*

The Cereus (see′-ree-us) tribe, with one hundred and thirteen genera and thousands of species and varieties, is the third, last, and most important tribe in the Cactus family. Its members may be recognized by their very succulent stems, which never show leaves except in the seedling stage, which bear spines but no glochids, and usually have funnel-shaped flowers with a long tube.

Because of its great size this tribe has been divided into eight subtribes. The first six subtribes have plants with stems and branches that have ribs, angles, or tubercles; their areoles generally bear spines; and their flowers have a long tube. The last two subtribes are epiphytic, or tree-dwelling, plants. Their stems and branches are generally spineless, flattened, weak, and drooping.

The Cereus tribe ranges from our extreme southern states through Mexico and Central America and the adjacent islands, south to Argentina and Chile. Its members are found from the seashore to altitudes of twelve thousand feet in the Andes. They range in height from one inch to sixty feet, and some species form many-branched, treelike plants weighing tons. The description, culture, and uses of these cacti are so varied that they must be discussed separately under each subtribe and genus.

The Torch Cacti—The Subtribe *Cereanae*

Members of this first and largest subdivision of the Cereus tribe have been called the Torch Cacti, for their stiff, upright stems often bear such a profusion of blooms that they look like torches aflame. There are forty-four genera in this subtribe, so varied in form and usefulness that it is best to describe them as belonging to one or another of four popular groups.

The first and largest, both in number and sheer physical size, are strong, ribbed columnar cacti which branch from thick stems to form a heavy treelike growth resembling giant candelabra. The second group are large columnar plants too, but branch from the base to resemble organ pipes. The third group are known as the Old Man Cacti because their strong columnar branches bear profuse hairs at their sides or tips. And the fourth group are relatively small, thin, clambering plants which might be called the Slender Torches.

The Candelabra Cacti. Of the large Candelabra Cacti those found in the genus *Cereus* are perhaps the most commonly grown. They are very large, strong-growing plants of easy culture that make splendid backgrounds in outdoor plantings where temperatures do not fall below 20° F. While these plants may reach sixty feet in a century or two and weigh tons, like their giant relative the Saguaro (sah-wah'-ro), *Carnegiea gigantea,* they are so beautiful and interesting as seedling plants that a place should be found for them in every collection. Such young plants are especially prized indoors for their beautifully colored stems and large, white, night-blooming flowers.

Perhaps the most popular species is the Peruvian Torch, *Cereus peruvianus,* a free-blooming plant with ribbed sea-green stems and brown or black spines. Another favorite is *C. dayamii,* unexcelled for its profuse blooms and large red fruit. And, finally, the very unusual *C. jamacaru,* whose young stems are a distinct blue green in contrast to its yellow spines and foot-long white blooms.

All the ten or more species in the Mexican genus *Pachycereus* (pak-ee-see'-ree-us) are also giant treelike plants, but young seedlings make very attractive potted specimens. They require a loose soil with considerable leaf mold added, plenty of water in warm weather, and a minimum temperature of

THE CACTUS FAMILY

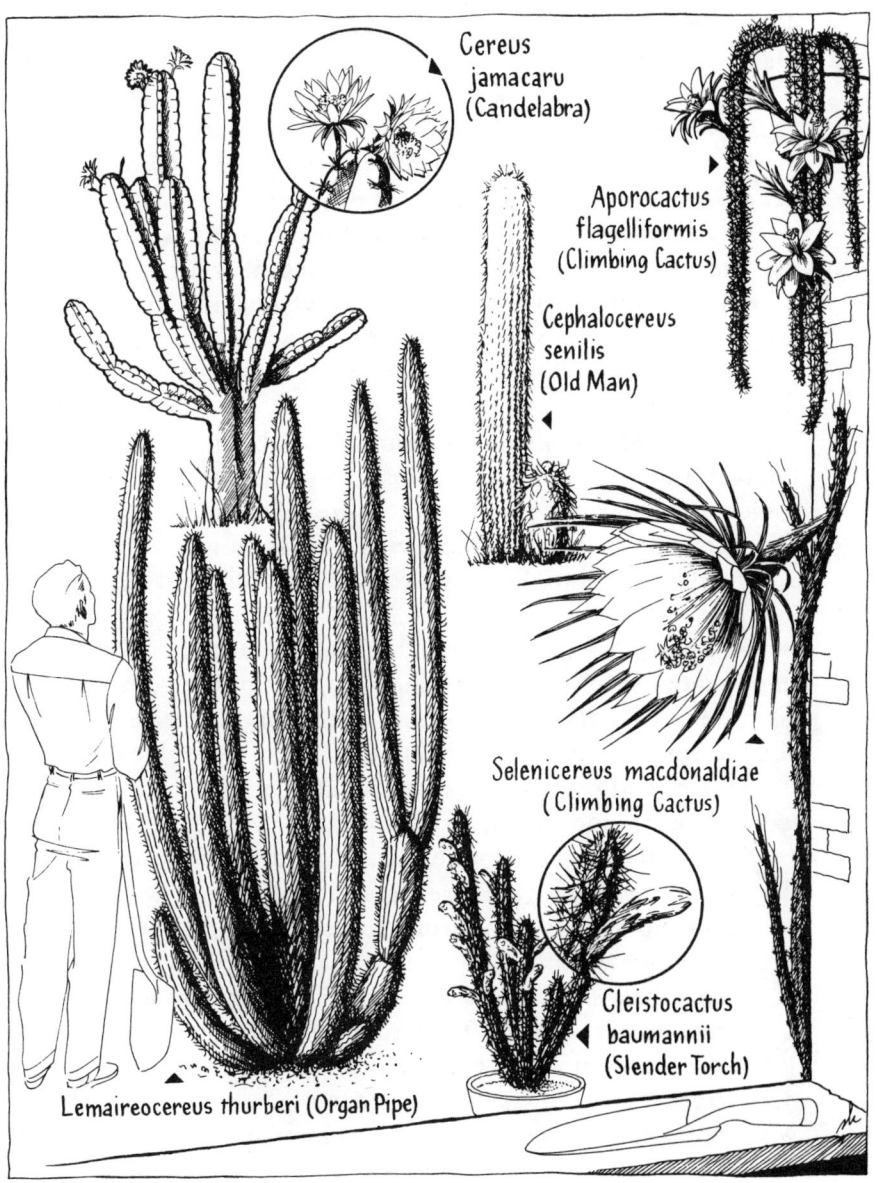

THE TORCH AND CLIMBING CACTI

40°F. *Pachycereus pringlei,* the Mexican Giant Cactus, with blackish-green fluted stems and numerous short gray spines, is probably the best-known species. But *P. pecten-aboriginum* is also noted for its extraordinarily spiny fruit, which resemble chestnut burs and are used by the Indians as combs, hence its popular name Indian Comb Cactus.

The genus *Stetsonia* (stet-so'-nee-ah) from northwestern Argentina contains only one treelike species, *S. coryne,* which makes a very decorative potted plant when small. Its dark gray-green, club-shaped stems bear long white radial spines that contrast beautifully with a formidable black central spine in each areole.

Myrtillocactus geometrizans (mur-til'-o-kak'-tus) is another popular Candelabra Cactus whose columnar branches are tinged with a bright bluish-white haze which turns smoky violet in winter. The prominent ribs bear short, stout spines and flowers that look like myrtle blossoms, followed by edible purple fruit.

The Organ Pipe Cacti. Unlike the giant Candelabra Cacti, those columnar species which branch from the base to form the Organ Pipe Cacti seldom exceed fifteen or twenty feet in height. But they are still relatively large plants, suitable only for background plantings, where climate permits, or as potted specimens indoors while still young.

Many of the popular species in the genus *Lemaireocereus* (le-may'-ro-see'-ree-us) are true Organ Pipe Cacti. They range in habitat from southern Arizona to Venezuela and the West Indies, and are exceptionally beautiful and interesting plants. A sunny location, liberal watering in summer, and a minimum temperature above 30°F. are all they require.

The best-known species is undoubtedly *L. marginatus,* a dark green columnar cactus with deeply fluted ribs edged with short white spines. *L. pruinosus* is another very easy and effective species covered with brown-black spines and a powdery blue bloom that gives it the common name Blue Mitre.

The Arizona Organ Pipe, *L. thurberi,* is a very popular species also, with heavy rounded ribs and brown to purple spines, but it is not so easy to grow in its seedling stage.

The unique forms and large white nocturnal flowers of the genus *Trichocereus* (trik-o-see'-ree-us) make it one of the most popular of the Organ Pipes for the beginning collector. These plants, native to the Andes from Chile to Ecuador, are exceptionally neat and easy to grow in the window garden or outdoors where temperatures remain above 20°F. *T. spachianus,* the White Torch Cactus, is as well known for its large snow-white flowers as it is as an understock for grafting other cacti. Somewhat similar and equally popular are *T. candicans* and *T. schickendantzii*—strong, short, columnar plants bearing fine white blooms.

The highly ornamental genus *Lophocereus* (lo-fo-see'-ree-us) is native to southern Arizona, Lower California, and Sonora. Its members are stout columnar cacti generally branching from the base. They are especially interesting because each areole on the flowering parts of the plant produces an extraordinary number of spines and two or more small, night-blooming pink flowers. They are of easy culture, especially the species *L. schottii.* A monstrose variety of this species, popularly called the Totem Pole Cactus, *L. schottii* var. *monstrosus,* is a knobby, ribless, spineless freak that seems to be carved out of green soap.

The Old Man Cacti. Probably more collections have been started by the attraction of these woolly-headed columnar cacti than all other kinds combined. Of the several genera and species of "Old Men" the most popular is easily the Mexican Old Man, *Cephalocereus senilis* (sef'-ah-loh-see'-ree-us), whose stout columnar body is completely covered with long snowy-white hairs. It is a "must" for every collection. Another very popular plant in this genus is the Golden Old Man, *C. chrysacanthus,* whose blue ribbed stems bear a profusion of bright yellow spines and masses of lighter wool.

In other genera the Peruvian Old Man, *Espostoa lanata* (es-po'-sto-ah), is a handsome, easily grown plant completely covered with white cottony hair. And equally popular is the Old Man of the Andes, *Oreocereus celsianus* (o'-ree-o-see'-ree-us), an exceptionally fine plant with stout brown spines and a head of wispy white hair.

The Slender Torches. The last group of plants in the subtribe *Cereanae* are quite unlike the large Candelabra and Organ Pipes or the stout Old Men. They are relatively thin, weak-stemmed plants whose great attraction lies not in imposing forms and handsome hair, but in the remarkable beauty and profusion of their blooms.

Some of the most prolific bloomers among all cacti are found in the several species of the genus *Monvillea* (mon-vil'-ee-ah), slender, long-stemmed, night-blooming cacti from South America. They are half-erect plants suitable for a mid-foreground position in landscaping or as fairly compact potted plants. *M. cavendishii* is perhaps the most prolific bloomer, and *M. spegazzinii* is especially prized for its beautiful blue marbled stems. The monvilleas require rather more leaf mold, shade, and warmth than most cacti, but are well worth the added care.

The Snake Cactus, *Nyctocereus serpentinus* (nik-toe-see'-ree-us), is another slender night bloomer whose large, fragrant white flowers are outstanding. The tall, graceful, columnar plants, studded with short red and gray spines, are easily grown and universally popular.

Another beautiful group of straight Slender Torch Cacti is found in the genus *Cleistocactus* (klice-toe-kak'-tus). The handsome Scarlet Bugler, *C. baumannii,* with its dark spines and bright tubular blooms, has been well loved for more than a century. And the Silver Torch, *C. strausii,* is a many-ribbed, slender beauty whose long spiny hairs give an illusion of soft, silvery silkiness to the plant. Very similar but with stouter branches and whiter spines is the popular White

Torch, *C. hyalacanthus*. All the cleistocacti are of the easiest culture, and can take temperatures to 20°F., but the white-spined species should be given somewhat less water than the others.

Perhaps the most striking flowers among the Slender Torches belong to the genus *Heliocereus* (hee'-lee-oh-see'-ree-us). These are clambering tropical plants, native to Mexico and Central America, whose spectacular day-blooming flowers are considered by many the finest in the Cactus family. The Sun Cereus, *H. speciosus,* is perhaps the best-known species. Its magnificent scarlet flowers have been extensively crossed with the epiphyllums to give us the so-called Orchid Cacti, or modern hybrid epiphyllums. The heliocerei appreciate generous soil and watering but, being tropical plants, will not take temperatures much below 50°F.

To conclude this list of Slender Torch Cacti we must add those almost vinelike plants of prolific blooming habit that make up the genus *Eriocereus* (ehr'-ee-oh-see'-ree-us). They are strong-growing cacti requiring rather large pots, rich soil, and abundant watering, and can take temperatures to 20°F. *E. bonplandii,* with huge white night flowers from spring until late fall, is probably the best-loved variety. But the Pink Moon Cactus, *E. regelii,* with very similar pink blooms, is a close rival.

The Climbing Cacti—The Subtribe *Hylocereanae*

After the sprawling vinelike growth of some of the Slender Torches, it is not surprising to find that the second subtribe of the Cereus tribe consists of true climbing cacti. All the *Hylocereanae* (hy-loh-see'-ree-ay'-nee) have thin stems, often reaching amazing lengths, and aerial roots by which they draw humidity from the air and cling to rocks or the bark of trees. These devices have permitted them to sometimes leave the ground entirely and become epiphytes (ep'-ee-fite), or tree dwellers, getting nourishment from the humus collected in the forks of trees without any contact with the soil below.

Perhaps the best known of the Climbing Cacti is *Hylocereus undatus* (hy-loh-see'-ree-us), whose three-winged stems bear the immense white nocturnal blooms pictured on the jacket of this book. It is a magnificent, easily grown, free-blooming plant that has been widely used for hedges in Hawaii and cultivated in other tropical countries for its fine fruit. Elsewhere it requires ample room espaliered on a trellis or the rafters of a greenhouse, rich soil and abundant watering, and temperatures not much below 50°F.

Another vinelike Climbing Cactus, but with slender ribbed stems, is the very popular *Selenicereus macdonaldiae* (see-lee'-ni-see'-ree-us). It shares with a score of other night-blooming cacti the well-deserved but much overused titles of Queen of the Night and Night-blooming Cereus. For sheer size and spectacle no other cactus can match its gold and white blossoms, often a foot in diameter and as much in length. Equally fine are the species *S. grandiflorus* and *S. pteranthus.* While somewhat more hardy than *Hylocereus,* the selenicerei do best when given ample room, generous treatment, and temperatures above 40°F.

The slender, whiplike stems of the Rat-tail Cactus, *Aporocactus flagelliformis* (ap'-oh-roh-kak'-tus), are much shorter than the other Climbing Cacti, yet they may reach three feet in length when grown as hanging-basket plants. It is for this graceful weeping habit and a profusion of bright red flowers in spring that it has been a favorite pot plant the world over. Occasionally it is grafted on tall nyctocereus or selenicereus understocks and trained over a framework to form a striking umbrella-shaped standard. The Rat-tail Cactus likes rich soil, abundant water when growing, and protection from the frost in winter.

THE CACTUS FAMILY

The Hedgehog Cacti—The Subtribe *Echinocereanae*

Unlike the slender, tropical, Climbing Cacti which make up the second subtribe of the Cereus clan, the members of the third subtribe are short, cylindrical, or globe-shaped desert or brushland plants, rarely a foot in height, usually heavily armed with spines, which produce their brilliantly colored flowers from areoles at the base and sides of their stems. They may be divided into two groups: the first, the Hedgehog Cacti of our Southwest and Mexico; and second, their several relatives from South America.

The largest and best-known genus is probably *Echinocereus* (ee-ky'-noh-see'-ree-us), native to our Southwest and Mexico, from whose name the whole subtribe gets its scientific as well as its popular name, Hedgehog Cacti. Popular species include *E. reichenbachii,* the Lace Cactus, so called because its numerous spines form a lacy cover over the plant; and *E. rigidissimus,* the Rainbow Cactus, a rather difficult plant to grow but highly prized for its multicolored spines, which form horizontal bands of pink, white, red, and brown. The flowers of both these species are purplish pink and quite large. Equally popular for its amazingly large yellow flowers is *E. dasyacanthus,* a short-spined, easily grown species. A very long-spined, pink-flowered species whose soft white hairs resemble the Mexican Old Man Cactus *(Cephalocereus senilis)* is *E. delaetii.* And to conclude the list every collection should include the handsome violet-red flowers of *E. pentalophus,* which are borne on a curious clustered plant with finger-like stems.

Because of their beautiful flowers, interesting spine growth, easy culture, and small size, virtually all the echinocerei make fine pot plants and can easily become a specialty with the collector. They are readily grown from seed or cuttings, require little water, and flower best when winter temperatures are kept above freezing, though many species are quite hardy.

Of the South American hedgehogs none has been more widely grown or loved than the genus *Echinopsis* (ek-ee-nop'-sis). Its many species are popularly called Easter Lily Cacti, because their small globular or cylindrical plants, heavily ribbed and spined, produce a wealth of large trumpet-shaped blooms of outstanding beauty. The flowers are generally pink or white and open in the evening and last through the next day until noon or later. The echinopses are of the easiest culture, preferring a rich soil, ample food and water in the growing season, and will take light shade. They are readily grown from seed and from the numerous offsets produced at the base of the plants. Several species, such as *E. multiplex,* are very hardy and have been used for bedding out of doors in sections of the United States and Canada where the plants are under snow all winter. They are extremely beautiful and free-flowering as potted plants, but when pink and white species are massed together out of doors in patterned beds they are simply spectacular.

Actually any and all available species of *Echinopsis* are desirable, but some of the most popular white-flowered kinds are *E. calochlora,* the Shining Ball, a handsome apple-green globular plant with short yellow spines and large white flowers; *E. eyriesii,* another fine white species; *E. huottii, E. silvestrii,* and *E. obrepanda.* Of the pink species the Pink Easter Lily Cactus, *E. multiplex,* is easily the most popular; but there are many other fine sorts, such as *E. campylacantha, E. oxygona,* and the Lilac Easter Lily Cactus, *E. rhodotricha* var. *argentinensis.* In addition to these species many fine new hybrids have been developed by crossing *Echinopsis* with the closely related lobivias and trichocerei. The resulting plants display the same fine flowers as the echinopses, but in a wide range of colors from salmon pink through orange and red.

There are three other genera of South American Hedgehog Cacti which are closely related to *Echinopsis* but differ from

THE CACTUS FAMILY

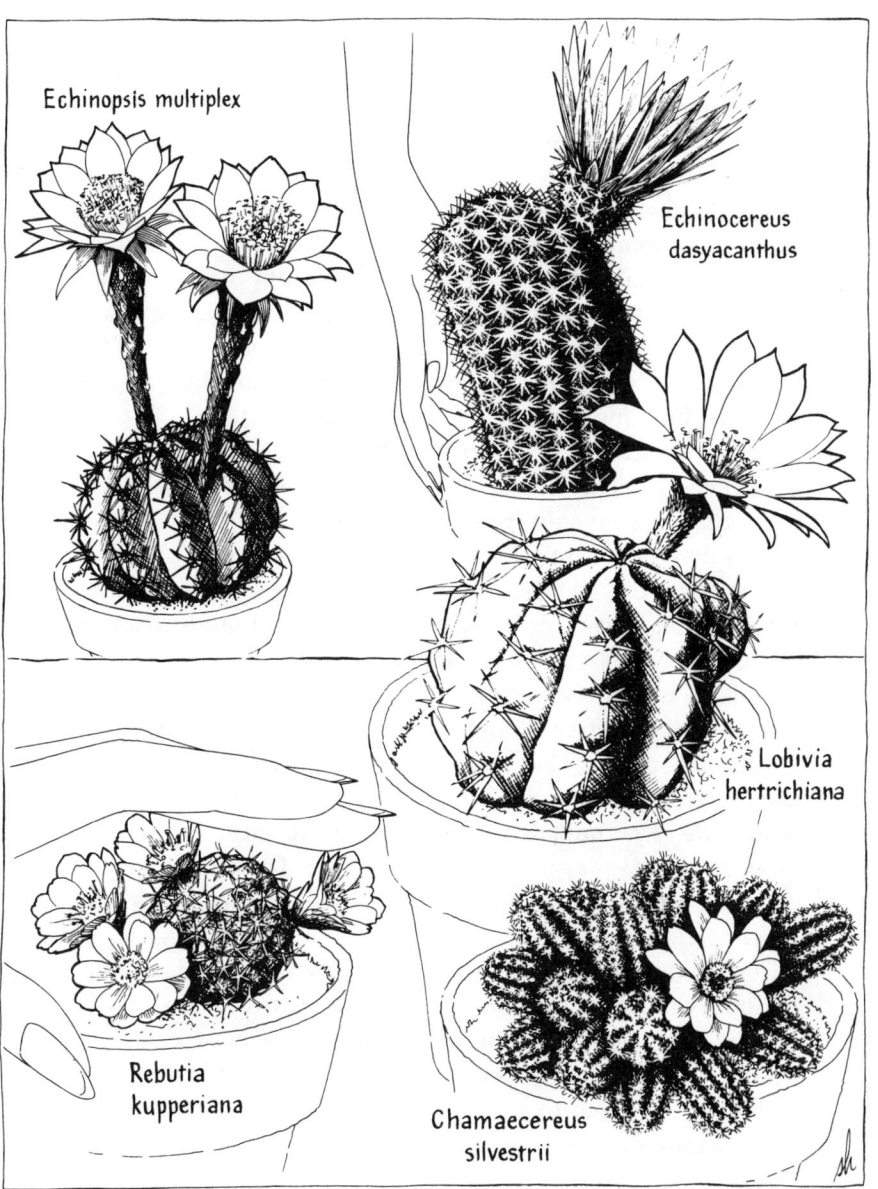

THE HEDGEHOG CACTI

it by having smaller plants, smaller flowers, and the habit of blooming by day. But despite their modest appearance they are among the most popular of all cacti for their brilliant silky flowers and small size, which makes them ideal pot plants.

The first of these are the lobivias (loh-biv′-ee-ah), short, cylindrical, spiny plants which are popularly called Cob Cacti. They are actually difficult to distinguish from the echinopses except their flowers have shorter tubes and open by day. The Golden Easter Lily Cactus, *L. aurea,* looks for all the world like a sparkling yellow echinopsis. Equally popular and free-blooming are the Orange Cob Cactus, *L. famatimensis;* the scarlet *L. hertrichiana;* and the lovely carmine *L. backebergii.* The lobivias are all very easily grown and can take considerable cold in winter.

Closely related to the lobivias but smaller in every way are the tiny rebutias (reh-boot′-ee-ah). They are no larger than a man's thumb, bear nipples instead of ribs, and produce a fantastic number of showy blooms in a circle near the base of the plant, which gives them the popular name Crown Cacti. Their small size, free-blooming, and easy culture make them ideal house plants. They require rather more water than most cacti and a partly shaded location indoors or out. *Rebutia minuscula* is perhaps the most popular species, with scarlet flowers often as large as the plant itself. Other fine species are the rosy-violet *R. violaciflora* and the dark red *R. kupperiana.*

Just as dainty as the rebutias are the tiny cylindrical stems of the Peanut Cactus, *Chamaecereus silvestrii* (kam-ee-see′-ree-us). This popular miniature cactus branches freely from the base to form clusters of peanut-shaped stems which are completely covered in spring with beautiful dark red flowers. The Peanut Cactus is quite hardy and easily grown out of doors in milder climates, where it revels in full sun and liberal watering. Its joints are easily detached and rooted, and they are sometimes also grafted on pereskia or cereus understock to form specimen plants. Although there is only one species of chamaecereus, it has been crossed with the lobivias to produce a number of fine free-flowering hybrids.

The Living Rock, Barrel, Star, Chin, and Ball Cacti—The Subtribe *Echinocactanae*

This fourth subtribe of the Cereus line is second largest in size, with thirty-seven genera, among which are found some of the real curiosities and novelties of the Cactus family. Although they range vastly in size and form, they may be differentiated from all preceding genera by one common characteristic: the flowers arise from young undeveloped areas in the center of the plant. The subtribe may be divided into five popular groups for easy recognition.

The Living Rock Cacti. The Living Rock Cacti are the mimicry plants of the Cactus family. With their curious rock-like forms and textures they have learned to protect themselves from the foragers of the southwestern and Mexican deserts they inhabit. Many of them have strong turnip-like roots by which they pull themselves into the soil in times of drought, blending even more closely with the soil and rocks. Because of their excellent camouflage they are as a rule practically spineless, only their tough skin and stonelike texture protect them. Most of them are slow-growing plants, sometimes a little difficult to keep and propagate, but wonderful novelties for any collection.

The most popular of these cacti is undoubtedly the Mexican Living Rock, *Ariocarpus fissuratus* (a'-ree-oh-kar'-pus), a curious plant made up of overlapping horny tubercles covered with a tough, leathery skin through which the underlying green shows faintly. The top of the plant is filled with gray wool out of which spring lovely pink blossoms. Along similar lines, yet distinct, are the Pine Cone Cactus, *Encephalo-*

carpus strobiliformis (en'-sef-ah-loh-kar'-pus), with violet-pink blooms; *Obregonia denegrii* (oh-bre-goh'-nee-ah), with lovely white flowers; *Strombocactus disciformis* (strom-boh-kak'-tus), and *Aztekium ritteri* (as-tek'-ee-um).

Three remarkable curiosities which may not really be classed as Living Rocks but which are no less amazing are the Dumpling Cactus, the Brain Cacti, and the Agave Cactus. The Dumpling Cactus, *Lophophora williamsii* (loh-fof'-oh-rah), is the well-known Peyote, from which the Indians extract the narcotic mescal, used in native religious ceremonies. It is a small, round, spineless plant with broad, flattened ribs—not especially interesting either for its appearance or small white or pink flowers, but rather for its use as "dry whiskey" by the Indians.

The Brain Cacti, on the other hand, are a distinct and beautiful genus with no close relatives. They get their popular name from the dozens of thin wavy ribs which run down the small, globular, spiny plants giving them a curiously wrinkled appearance. The pretty pink, purple, or white bell-shaped blooms are usually attractively striped and freely produced. *Stenocactus* or, as it is sometimes called, *Echinofossulocactus multicostatus* (ee-ky'-noh-fos'-oo-loh-kak'-tus) is perhaps the best-known species, but is more difficult to grow than many other species which are generally as desirable and of very easy culture.

The Agave Cactus, *Leuchtenbergia principis* (loik-ten-berg'-ee-ah) is really one of the great oddities in the Cactus family. From a large taproot a group of long finger-like tubercles arise, each ending in a woolly areole. From these areoles come thin papery spines and large, yellow, fragrant flowers which last several days. The long, angled, blue-green tubercles and loose rosette form of this unique plant actually make it look more like an agave than a cactus.

The Barrel Cacti. The Barrel Cacti are perhaps best known for the widespread notion that parched desert travelers can

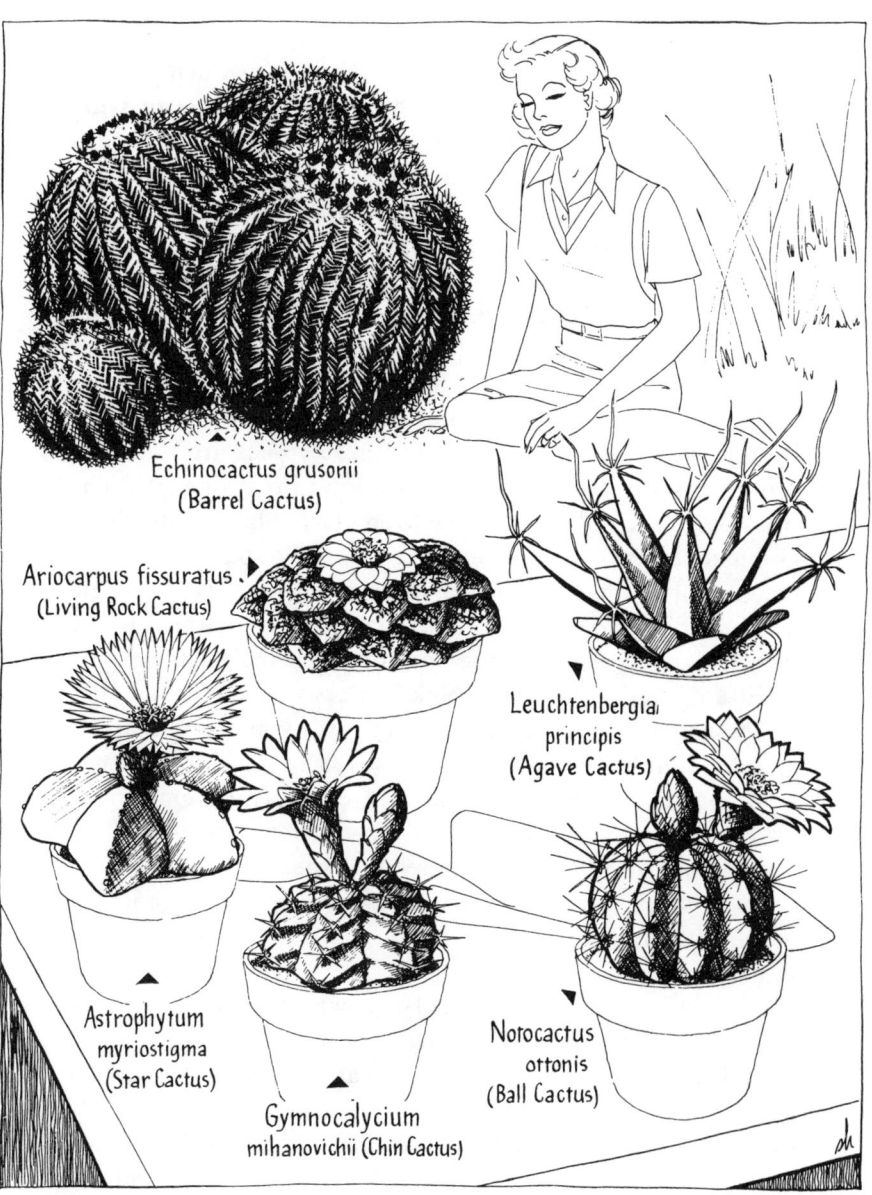

THE LIVING ROCK, BARREL, STAR, CHIN, AND BALL CACTI

get water simply by tapping these barrel-shaped reservoirs. It is true that the very juicy pulp of these cacti when mashed and pounded will yield a mucilaginous drink, but no one dying of thirst is likely to have the strength either to make this "water" or stomach it. Actually the Mexicans have found two slightly more practical uses for these Barrel Cacti. From the strong, hooked spines of some species they make fishhooks, and from the juicy pulp, flavored and boiled in sugar, they make the insipid "cactus candy" so attractive to tourists.

Of all Barrel Cacti the most popular is undoubtedly the magnificent Golden Barrel, *Echinocactus grusonii* (ee-ky'-noh-kak'-tus), a bright green globe with very long, stiff yellow spines. When the plant is young, these spines are borne on prominent nipples, which later develop into strong ribs. The Blue Barrel, *E. ingens,* is also extremely popular as its bluish globular body develops attractive purple bands when it reaches three or more inches in diameter. Another old favorite is *E. horizonthalonius,* the Eagle Claw Cactus, with its heavy recurved pink or red spines set off by a pale silvery-gray plant and handsome frilled pink flowers in summer.

The genus *Ferocactus* (fee-ro-kak'-tus), which contains the greatest number of Barrel Cacti, is well represented by such stout barrels as *F. latispinus,* with intertwined clusters of broad, hooked spines topped by a crown of ribbon-like dark pink spines and blossoms. Other fine species are the Giant-spined Barrel, *F. rectispinus,* with hatpin spines to ten inches in length; the Fishhook Barrel, *F. wislizenii; F. nobilis,* and *F. alamosanus.*

The Barrel Cacti are all easily grown from seed, but they take years to make mature flowering plants as they grow to immense size and weight. They are attractive balls of spines when young, but become broadly cylindrical with age, heavily ribbed, and eventually require considerable room. These cacti are perhaps most successful planted out of doors and are quite frost-resistant if properly hardened by reduced watering in fall and winter.

The Star Cacti. Although the Star Cacti belong to a very small Mexican genus containing only four species, their unusual beauty and easy culture have made them universally popular. The plants are usually globular, with a few very prominent ribs more or less covered with white scales, which make them appear as though dusted with powder. The large yellow flowers appear near the top of the plants followed by very woolly fruit.

Of all the Star Cacti the Bishop's Cap, *Astrophytum myriostigma* (as-tro-fy'-tum), is perhaps most popular and aptly named; for it is a smooth, white, spineless plant divided by five fluted ribs and crowned with yellow flowers through the summer. *A. asterias,* the Sand Dollar, is a much rarer spineless species that more nearly resembles a sea urchin than a cactus, until it opens its beautiful yellow blossoms stained red in the throat. But the handsomest yellow and red flowers of all are borne by *A. capricorne,* the Goat's Horn, a smooth globular plant flecked with white whose spiraled ribs bear twisted, hornlike, papery spines reminiscent of the Paperspined Opuntia. And, finally, no collection should be without the handsome and easily grown Star Cactus *A. ornatum,* a slightly taller species whose fluted body is richly ornamented with starlike silvery scales, sharp spines, and lemon-yellow blossoms.

The Chin Cacti. The gymnocalyciums (jim'-noh-ka-lis'-ee-um), or Chin Cacti, are especially recommended to beginners for their easy culture, beautiful long-lasting flowers, and interestingly shaped plants. They are generally very small globular cacti whose ribs bear curious protuberances, or "chins," under each areole, hence their popular name. The most popular species is undoubtedly the Plaid Cactus, *G. mihanovichii,* a small plant with attractively banded ribs and abundant pale yellow to chartreuse flowers. Even more beautiful in bloom are the White Chin, *G. schickendantzii;* Dam's Chin, *G. damsii,* with white flowers tinged pink; the Pink Chin, *G. fleischerianum;* the bright red *G. venturianum;* and the Dwarf Chin, *G. quehlianum.* In fact, almost any of the Chin Cacti are sure to bloom easily and profusely, sometimes when they are no larger than an inch in diameter.

The Ball Cacti. Among other small cacti prized for easy and prolific blooming one must not overlook the Ball Cacti. Plants of the genus *Notocactus* (noh-toe-kak'-tus) are popular for their small size, brightly colored spines, and large showy flowers. They are of easiest culture, and will take temperatures to 20°F. Some attractive species are the Sun Cup, *N. apricus,* with soft gray spines and large yellow blossoms; the Golden Ball, *N. leninghausii,* a ball of soft golden spines and lemon-yellow flowers; the Silver Ball, *N. scopa,* similar, but with a coat of beautiful silvery-white spines; the Indian Head, *N. ottonis,* with glittering yellow blooms from spring till fall; and the Lemon Ball, *N. submammulosus,* a very free yellow bloomer.

Very like the notocacti are the parodias (pa-roh'-dee-ah), a charming group of small, free-blooming cacti ideal for the window-sill collection. The best known is the popular Tom Thumb Cactus, *P. aureispina,* a tiny golden-spined cactus that never gets much bigger than a tennis ball and bears large orange flowers when scarcely an inch in diameter. Equally interesting are *P. mutabilis,* with yellow blossoms, and the brilliant Crimson Parodia, *P. sanguiniflora.*

The Melon Cacti—The Subtribe *Cactanae*

While the plants in this fifth subtribe are among the most unusual in the Cactus family and of especial historical interest because they were among the first cacti to be introduced to Europe, they are generally so slow in cultivation that they

THE CACTUS FAMILY

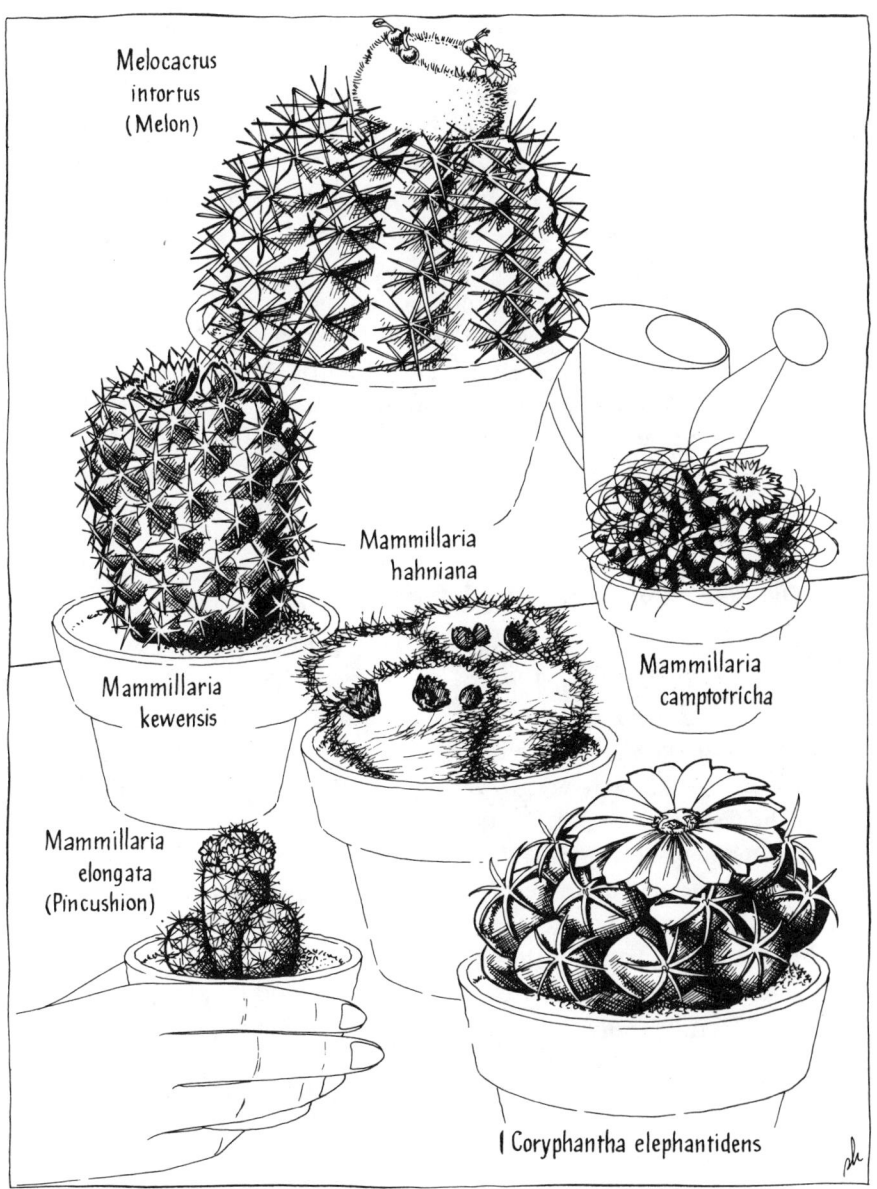

THE MELON AND PINCUSHION CACTI

are virtually useless to the beginning collector. There are two tropical genera, *Discocactus* (dis-ko-kak'-tus) and *Melocactus* (mel-oh-kak'-tus), and they can be distinguished from all other cacti by the fact that their flowers arise from a headlike mass of wool and bristles called a cephalium (seh-fay'-lee-um), which sits on top the plant. This head is so distinct from the melon-shaped body of the plant that it looks as if it had been grafted to it. In *Melocactus intortus,* for example, the body of the plant resembles a Barrel Cactus, but it is topped with a striking red or brown head which looks so much like a fez that the plant is popularly called the Turk's Cap Cactus. The Melon Cacti are strictly greenhouse plants for the expert grower. They require heat, perfect drainage, very moderate watering, and considerable age to develop their striking form.

The Pincushion Cacti—The Subtribe *Coryphanthanae*

In all the Cactus family no other cacti have been so widely grown and loved as house plants as the Pincushion Cacti. Their small size, abundant jewel-like flowers, bright fruit, and easy culture have made them so popular with amateurs that many are content to grow them alone in preference to all other cacti.

Of the sixteen genera in this subtribe two are outstanding, *Mammillaria* (mam-ee-lay'-ree-ah) and *Coryphantha* (koh-ree-fan'-tha). They are distinguished from other members of the Cereus tribe in having lines of tubercles or nipples *(mamillae)* instead of ribs, and from the other members of the Cactus family in having the spine-producing and flower-producing centers of their areoles separated. In the genus *Mammillaria,* for example, the flowers do not arise from the spiny areole which tips each tubercle, but from a generally hairy or woolly areole which lies between the older tubercles at the top of the plant. In other genera, such as *Coryphantha,* these divided centers are joined by a pronounced groove on the upper side of each young tubercle, from the base of which the flowers arise. The mammillarias may be further distinguished because half their species possess normal watery sap and the other half a milky sap—a feature not found in any other member of the Cactus family.

Most of the nearly three hundred species of *Mammillaria* are native to Mexico, with a scattering of species in our Southwest, Central America, and the Caribbean. They range from the seashore to eight thousand feet, growing exposed on high mesas, beneath desert shrubs, on sheer canyon walls, and in rocky washes. Some are solitary plants, others form clusters or great mounds containing hundreds of plants. They vary in size from tiny globular plants an inch high to cylindrical forms a foot high, but all of them are delightfully neat, compact plants. The beautiful colors of their spines (white, yellow, red, black, or gray), in a variety of intricate patterns (straight, hooked, feathery, silky, or starred), vie with the bright circle of tiny flowers which crown the plants and ripen into brilliant fruit. And, to top it all, the mammillarias are of the easiest culture, ideal miniature cacti for the crowded window sill, greenhouse, or succulent border.

Of the hundreds of species available, almost all of which are desirable, a few universal favorites must be mentioned. Two delightful miniature species are the Thimble Cactus, *M. fragilis,* which bears at the top of its thimble-sized cylindrical body a profusion of baby plants; and *M. elongata,* a tiny columnar plant, branching from the base, whose clusters of bright yellow radial spines have won for it the familiar name Golden Stars. Equally popular are several species with feathery or silky spines. The Powder Puff Cactus, *M. bocasana,* is a dainty globular plant with soft, fluffy white hair, creamy flowers, and tiny bright red fruit. Somewhat similar is the very beautiful Feather Cactus, *M. plumosa,* whose feathery white spines completely cover the plant. The Silken Pincushion, *M. bombycina,* is a very handsome species with white radial and fishhook spines, a snowy head of wool, and deep pink flowers. But the queen of them all is the Old Lady Cactus, *M. hahniana,* a spectacular Pincushion covered with very long white hair and brilliant violet-red blossoms in winter.

Of the hundreds of species which remain—each notable in its own way for the shape and pattern of its spines, color of its flowers, or abundance of its fruit—we might select the following at random. Among the clustering types any collection would be enhanced by the Mother of Hundreds, *M. compressa;* the Bird's Nest Cactus, *M. camptotricha;* the Snowball Pincushion, *M. candida;* or the ever popular Owl's Eyes, *M. parkinsonii.* Of the tall-growing, solitary Pincushions one should not miss *M. vaupelii, M. kewensis,* or *M. spinosissima.* The mammillarias provide an inexhaustible treasure of forms and varieties for the collector, of which, once he has started to collect, he is never likely to have enough.

The genus *Coryphantha* consists of plants which are very similar to the mammillarias, except that they have much larger flowers and usually longer taproots. When grown in pots they should be given somewhat deeper containers, or if the taproot is extremely long it may be cut back to within an inch of the plant base, which should then be dried for two weeks and rerooted.

Of the globular species the most sought after is *C. elephantidens,* a strong-growing plant with curved brown spines and four-inch pink flowers. Somewhat similar, but with smaller yellow flowers, are the popular *C. bumamma* and *C. radians.* Among tall-growing, cylindrical species *C. erecta* is especially favored for its handsome golden-yellow spines; and so is *C. clava,* which offers in addition very large, pale yellow blossoms in summer. But perhaps the easiest, most free-flowering species of all is *C. macromeris* from Texas, with its large, deep purple blooms.

The Tree-dwelling Cacti—The Subtribes *Epiphyllanae* and Rhipsalidanae

In the second subtribe, the *Hylocereanae,* we found a group of Climbing Cacti which, while usually rooted in the ground, sometimes fastened themselves by aerial roots to the trunks and branches of trees and learned to live on the mosses and litter there. But in these last two subtribes of the Cactus family we have plants which are completely tree-dwelling, having taken as their home the high branches of the tropical forests. We call these cacti epiphytes, for like their jungle neighbors —the orchids and bromeliads—they get their nourishment through their aerial roots and from the leaf mold and mosses in the crotches of the trees they inhabit. They are not parasites, because they simply live *on* trees not *from* them.

The Epiphyllanae. The most important of these tree-dwelling cacti are members of the subtribe *Epiphyllanae* (ep'-ee-fe-lay'-nee). All seven genera are native to tropical Mexico, the West Indies, Central and South America. Their branches are flat, leaflike, usually scalloped along the edges, with a virtually spineless areole in each indentation. Each plant bears a number of these flat branches linked together by strong woody midribs, and they resemble cascading chains of leaves. The flowers are usually large and showy, mostly night-blooming, and are borne on the sides of the stems.

Of the seven genera one, the genus *Epiphyllum* (ep-ee-fil'-um), is outstanding. There are about twenty species, most of which are interesting for their very long, beautifully scalloped stems; usually large white night-blooming flowers; and sweet edible fruit. Collectors especially favor the very deeply notched, fernlike stems of *E. anguliger;* the very popular fragrant *E. latifrons,* grown on so many porches as a "Night-blooming Cereus"; *E. strictum,* a very dainty white flower with vivid crimson pistil; and the day-blooming *E. crenatum*, a wonderful basket plant with six-inch white blooms.

But actually it is for the thousands of hybrid epiphyllums that this genus is particularly noted. Nowhere else in the Cactus family have hybridists made such unbelievable progress, crossing the relatively modest epiphyllum species with such distant relatives as *Heliocereus* and *Selenicereus* to give us a race of day-blooming cacti of incredible size and beauty. In the attempt to somehow describe these spectacular blooms they have been given the popular name Orchid Cacti, but there are no orchids on earth that can compare in size, color, texture, and beauty with these modern hybrid epiphyllums. And, best of all, they are wonderfully easy plants to grow, ideal basket or espalier plants for the porch or greenhouse, lath house or garden.

Among the three thousand or more named epiphyllum hybrids now grown, the beginner can find almost any size, shape, color, and texture imaginable. But if he wishes a dozen standard varieties, tried and true, he can do no better than select these universal favorites. For their pure white petals backed by bronze and sulphur sepals, exceptionally free bloom, and flowers eight to ten inches in diameter, Eden and Oriole are perhaps the two most popular white varieties. In pink we have the starlike Padre and the handsome lilac Latona. And for sheer brilliance nothing can match the prodigal scarlet blooms of Vive Rouge or the nine-inch Scarlet Giant. But the ultimate in dazzling beauty is reached in the multicolored Hermosissimus, an unbelievable blend of orange, violet, and red; and the superb Friedrich Werner-Beul, a ten-inch red-purple with each petal bordered white. Another heroic bloom is Sun Goddess, in molten gold and violet with a vermilion eye; and Gloria, a prodigious bloomer in soft orange amber. And, for good measure, every collection should include the ever popular crimson and violet Conway's Giant and the dainty pink Rosetta, whose four-inch rosebud flowers and neat

THE CACTUS FAMILY

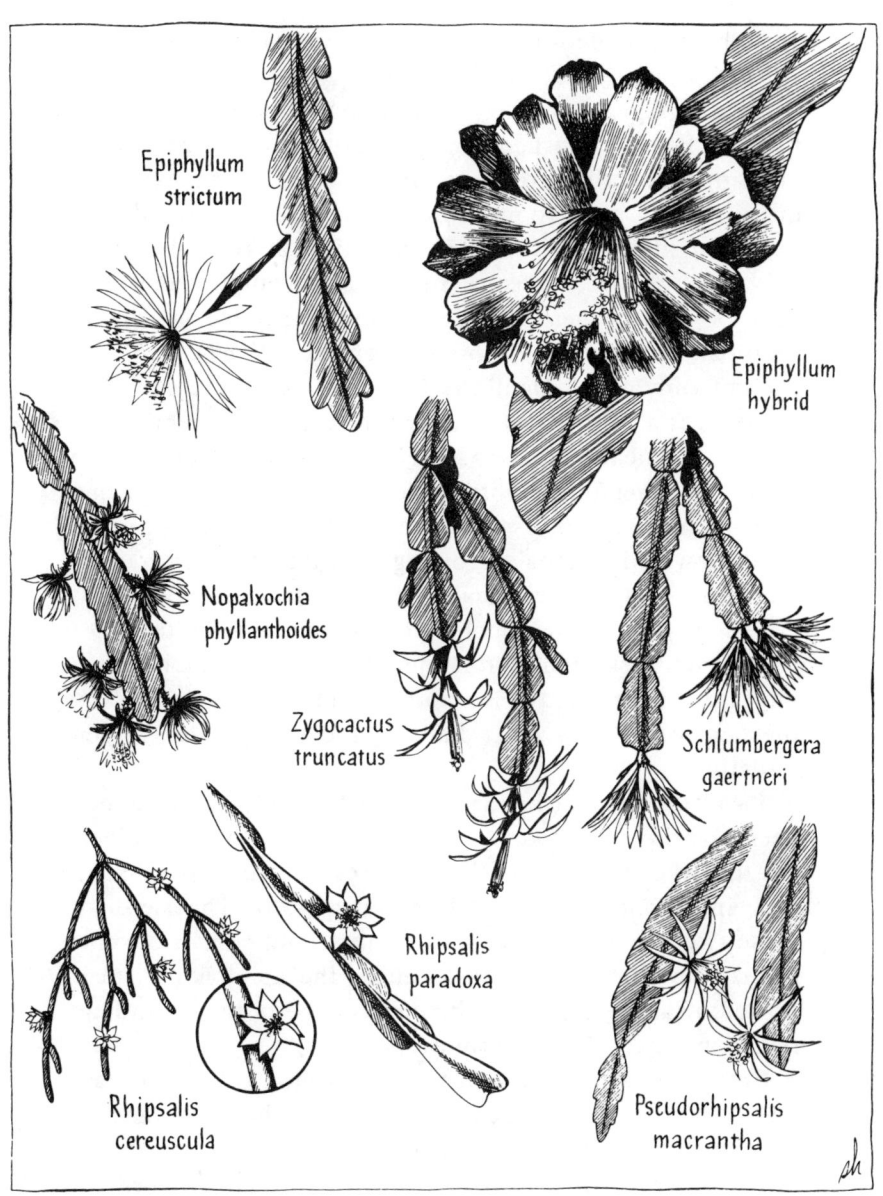

THE TREE-DWELLING CACTI

growth have made it a favorite basket plant the world over.

The popularity of small-flowered, compact plants like Rosetta has given rise to a whole new race of epiphyllum hybrids. Because most epiphyllum varieties are large, strong-growing plants they are rather awkward as house plants, requiring much more room than the average window-sill gardener can afford to give. In the past his only recourse was to grow one of the smaller relatives of the epiphyllums. The most popular of these is undoubtedly the genus *Nopalxochia* (noh-pal-soh'-chee-ah), whose only species, *N. phyllanthoides,* is commonly called Deutsche Kaiserin, or Empress of Germany. It is a very dainty plant with charming rosebud-pink flowers and neat branches, scarcely one sixth as large as the common epiphyllum hybrids. With this genus as a starting point hybridizers have now developed a whole new race of small-flowered, compact-growing epiphyllums that are perfect house plants. They come in every conceivable color and are, if anything, even more free-blooming than their big cousins. Of these miniature epiphyllum hybrids the beginner might try the fuchsia-red Bambi, the brilliant pink Sea Breeze, the fiery orange-red Peter Pan, or the multishaded-salmon Ballerina.

Two other genera in the subtribe *Epiphyllanae* have long been favorite house plants, though they are somewhat different than the epiphyllums. They are *Zygocactus* (zy-goh-kak'-tus) and *Schlumbergera* (shlum-ber'-ger-ah). The stems of these two genera are very flat, narrow, and consist of short leaflike links in long chains. Unlike the epiphyllums, their flowers usually appear at the ends of the branches and are relatively small but very profuse.

From the basic species *Zygocactus truncatus*—with irregular, deep rose, fuchsia-like flowers—several hundred varieties have been developed over the years ranging from pure white to deep purple. Because most of these bloom in December they have been given the popular name Christmas Cactus, but they are also sometimes known as Crab Cactus because the individual links of their stems resemble a clawed crab in outline.

Although plants of the genus *Schlumbergera* look very much like zygocacti, their flowers are not irregular and reflexed but open and wheel-shaped, with pointed petals. The species *S. gaertneri,* with rich scarlet flowers, is most commonly grown, and as it blooms in early spring it is popularly called the Easter Cactus. Both *Zygocactus* and *Schlumbergera* in their several varieties and hybrids are outstanding small plants for the home or greenhouse. They may be grown in pots, hanging baskets, or grafted to a short trunk of selenicereus to form miniature treelike specimens.

The Rhipsalidanae. It is sometimes very difficult for the novice to accept the plants in this last subtribe as members of the Cactus family. They are all tree dwellers, and form great pendent masses, with stems ranging from thin pencil-like forms to flat, leaflike links such as we encountered in the *Epiphyllanae.* Their flowers are very small, white to pink, and are followed by purple or white berries which resemble gooseberries.

Of the eight genera only one, *Rhipsalis* (rip'-sah-lis), is common in amateur collections. They are very easy and interesting plants, but are grown more for their cascading form than for their insignificant flowers. Of the cylindrical species the Mistletoe Cactus, *R. mesembryanthemoides;* the Rice Cactus, *R. cereuscula;* and the Link Cactus, *R. paradoxa,* with its curiously three-angled stems, are quite popular. Among the flat, leafy types the Snowdrop Cactus, *R. houlletiana;* the beautifully waved *R. crispata;* and the closely related *Pseudorhipsalis macrantha* (seu-doh-rip'-sah-lis), with its relatively large fragrant blossoms, are outstanding.

And so the Cactus family comes full circle. From the Eocene jungles through the deserts and wastelands back to the jungle again.

CHAPTER FOUR

Other Succulent Families

While the cacti were developing on our continent, many other plant families caught up in the vast changes of the Eocene were becoming succulents too. In the New World and Old many familiar plants using the same devices, to meet the same problems, took on strikingly similar forms.

At first this parallel development of widely different plants in widely separated continents may seem incredible. But when one remembers that there are only a limited number of solutions to the basic problems of sustaining life in the wastelands it is not surprising that many plants in many different places should have hit upon the same solutions again and again, and in doing so come to look very much alike.

Sometimes the changes in these lilies, amaryllids, and daisies have been so great that we might never guess their identity were it not for one infallible clue. No matter how much their outward appearance has changed in the process of becoming succulent, their flowers have remained much the same structurally as other members of their family. And with this clue we are able to discover some surprising succulent relatives of the common plants in our homes and gardens.

The Amaryllis Family—The *Amaryllidaceae*

Strange as it may seem, the amaryllis bulb blooming in your window, with its green strap-shaped leaves and wide trumpet flowers, has one very well-known succulent relative: the Century Plant. This most important succulent member of the Amaryllis family belongs to the genus *Agave* (ah-gah'-vee), whose more than three hundred species range from the southwestern United States to the equator and throughout the West Indies.

The agaves are succulent rosette plants varying in size from large specimens six or eight feet across, with bloom spikes thirty-five feet high, to handsome small species only a foot in diameter. Their flowers are usually yellow green and not especially colorful, but the bold form of the plants is very striking and decorative. The tough fibrous leaves of several species produce sisal, which is used in making rope, and the sap from the heart of other species is fermented to make the Mexican drink *pulque*.

Of the large agaves *A. americana,* the Century Plant, is certainly the most popular and commonly grown. Its broad, gray-green, lance-shaped leaves edged with dark brown teeth and tipped with a strong spine have developed a number of striking variegated forms, such as the variety *marginata,* with leaves edged yellow, and the varieties *medio-picta* and *striata,* with yellow stripes in the center of their leaves. But despite a popular misconception these Century Plants do not take a century to bloom, only ten to fifty years, after which they die, leaving numerous offsets at the base. With these offsets one can make handsome container plants that will remain relatively small for years.

Among the medium-sized species the soft gray-green rosettes of *A. attenuata* are truly outstanding. Broad, un-

OTHER SUCCULENT FAMILIES

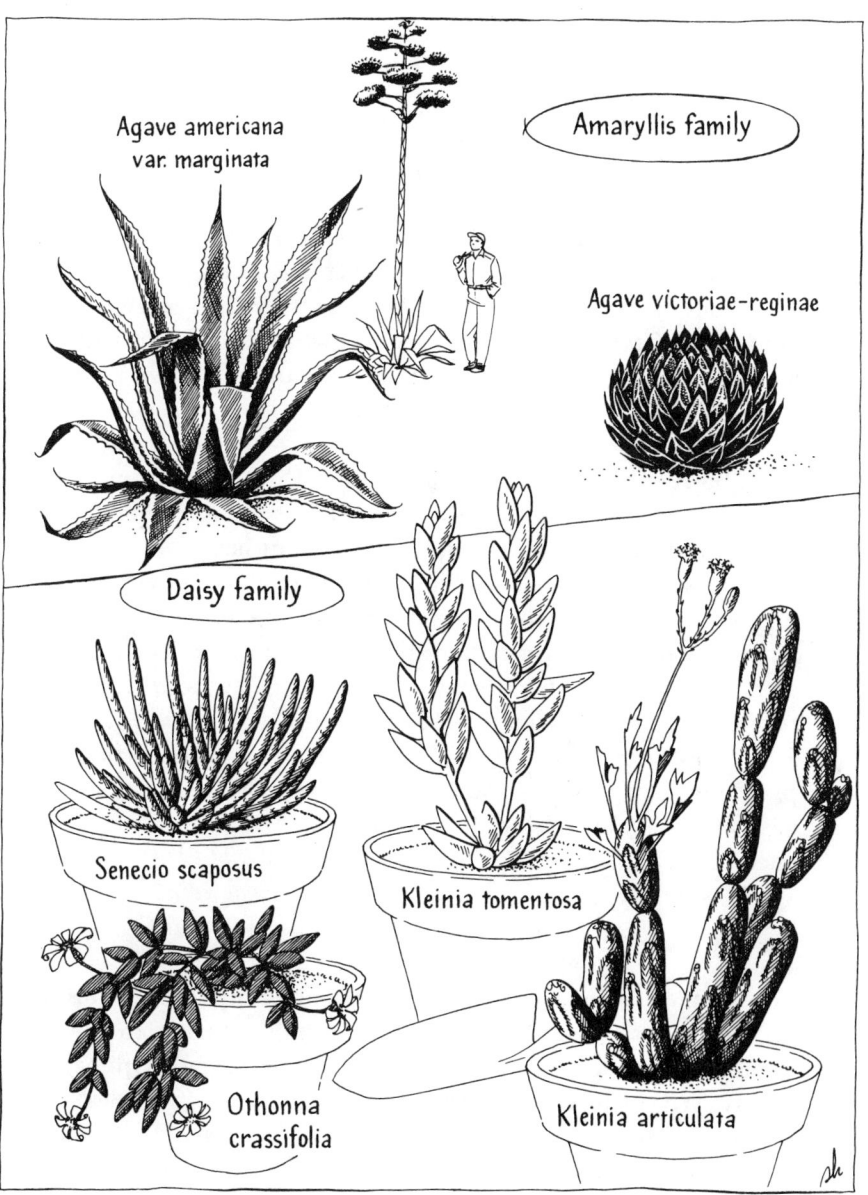

THE AMARYLLIS AND DAISY FAMILIES

armed, almost tropical in appearance, they have recently found wide use in landscaping and in containers with other ornamental foliage plants. In striking contrast, the leaves of *A. stricta,* the Hedgehog Agave, are scarcely a half inch wide, stiff, and sharply pointed to make a bristling rosette two feet across.

Of the small agaves *A. victoriae-reginae* is unquestionably the finest. Its narrow olive-green leaves, beautifully penciled and marked with white along the edges, form a compact globe of unbelievable symmetry. Somewhat similar, but with each leaf bearing loose curled threads along its margins, is the very popular and decorative *A. filifera.*

Although the agaves are perhaps the most familiar of all succulents other than cacti, they are not nearly so popular with collectors as they deserve to be. Perhaps long familiarity with the fierce, space-grabbing Century Plant has given a bad name to the whole clan, but there are many fine slow-growing species which no collection can afford to be without. The larger kinds make striking landscape specimens where sufficient room is available, and the smaller ones excellent potted plants for the patio, porch, or greenhouse. And, best of all, the agaves are rugged plants. They have no cultural problems except protection from freezing in winter, and are easily propagated by seed, offsets from the base of some species, or bulbils formed on the flower stalks of others.

The Crassula Family—The Crassulaceae

No other succulent family, except perhaps the Cactus, has contributed so many beautiful and familiar plants to our homes and gardens as the Crassula (kras'-eu-lah), or Orpine, family. With nearly a thousand species—all more or less leaf-succulent—it presents a bewildering range of forms, from large treelike shrubs to tiny plants only a fraction of an inch high. While some members of the family have very striking flowers, most of them are prized for their curious forms and highly decorative leaves. These fleshy leaves are sometimes attached to the stems alternately, in pairs at right angles to each other, or held in tight rosettes. Their surfaces are usually covered with wax or hairs, and are often beautifully marked and colored.

The twenty-five or more genera in the Crassula family are so widely scattered throughout the world and so diverse in form and habit that they have been divided into six major tribes as follows:

The Cotyledon Tribe. There are two important genera in this first tribe which have been known for a long time by the common name *Cotyledon* (kot-i-lee'-dun). But recently the smaller cotyledons with narrow, erect flowers have been grouped into a new genus called *Adromischus* (ad-ro-mis'-kus).

These miniature cotyledons, of which there are more than twenty species, are all native to Namaqualand and Cape Province in South Africa. Although they are tiny plants, only an inch or two high with very inconspicuous flowers, they are highly prized for their thick, alternate leaves, which are beautifully shaped and colored. Every collection should include *Adromischus cristatus,* whose tiny crested leaves and red stems, hairy with aerial roots, have given it the popular name Sea Shells. And equally fine are the compact clusters of fat, club-shaped, silver-green leaves of *A. clavifolius,* so often called Pretty Pebbles. But perhaps the best loved of all are the spotted species such as *A. maculatus,* whose thick, flat leaves marked chocolate brown are called Leopard's Spots; and *A. cooperi,* whose tiny egg-shaped leaves spotted maroon red are known the world over as Plover's Eggs. Actually any and all species of adromischus make perfect potted plants for the beginner because of their small size, beautiful colors, and exquisite forms.

The larger-growing genus *Cotyledon* contains more than thirty species, all native to South Africa, Abyssinia, and southern Arabia. These cotyledons are usually strong plants forming bold clumps, or even shrubs, and are as much admired for the exceptional form and color of their leaves as for their large clusters of pendent flowers in bright yellow, red, and green.

There are two classes of cotyledon: those with persistent leaves, and those like *C. cacalioides,* which develop a new rosette of leaves each year only to shed them in their summer resting period. Since these deciduous types are not especially attractive and rather difficult to propagate from cuttings, they are rarely grown. But all the other species are very popular.

Perhaps the best known are those shrubby kinds which have thick rounded leaves heavily powdered with a beautiful white bloom. Here we find *C. orbiculata,* a three-foot shrub with frosty leaves margined red; *C. ausana,* a dwarf species scarcely half as large but with very white leaves and bright orange-red blooms; and, best of all, *C. undulata,* whose broad snowy leaves, beautifully waved and fluted along the margins, have won for it the popular name Silver Crown.

In marked contrast to these shrubby white-leaved species are several low-growing cotyledons with quite small, fleshy, pointed leaves. *C. teretifolia* is probably the most popular and distinct of these, with its clusters of erect, dark green, hairy, cylindrical leaves and pale yellow flowers in summer.

All these popular species of adromischus and cotyledon are of the easiest culture, with no special requirements as to soil or water. But in order not to spoil the powdery white bloom on the leaves of some of them it is best not to water overhead. All members of this tribe develop their best form and color by getting as much air, warmth, and sunlight as possible, but many can stand considerable frost in winter. They are all easily propagated by seed or, better still, by leaf or stem cuttings in spring.

The Crassula Tribe. Of the five known genera in this second tribe of the *Crassulaceae* only two are commonly grown—the genus called *Crassula* and the genus *Rochea* (ro'-she-ah)—both natives of South Africa. These are usually small- to medium-sized plants with fleshy, opposing leaves arranged in such a way that each pair forms a cross in relation to its neighbors. Sometimes these leaves are closely packed on the stems, sometimes spaced well apart. The flowers are rather small, but occasionally very bright and forming large clusters.

Although the genus *Crassula* contains more than two hundred species, with a bewildering variety of forms and habits, it may be divided into two fairly distinct groups. The first consists of plants with visible branching stems that form good-sized shrubs, the other very small, low plants with the stem virtually hidden by the closely packed leaves.

Of the shrubby species the largest and best known is undoubtedly the Jade Plant, *C. argentea,* whose bright green rubbery leaves and dainty pink winter flowers make it one of the most familiar and widely grown succulents in the world. A variegated form of this species, with the leaves striped pink, cream, and green, is popularly known as the Tricolor Jade Plant. In mild climates the Jade Plant almost becomes a small tree, just as the popular *C. arborescens,* another large shrubby species with beautiful silvery leaves heavily dotted and margined with red. A much smaller shrub, though nearly as much grown, is *C. tetragona,* the so-called Midget Pine Tree, with short, dark green, pointed leaves arranged in four rows on stiff, upright stems. But none of these shrubby species can match the brilliant blooms of *C. falcata,* whose large trusses of scarlet flowers have given it the name Scarlet Paint Brush; and whose curiously twisted, silvery, two-ranked leaves have been dubbed Aeroplane Propellers. One other small, shrubby species especially noteworthy for its curious foliage is *C. perforata,* whose opposing pairs of leaves are joined together at the base, and so look as if threaded on the stems, hence its popular name String of Buttons.

Among the low-growing species no collection should miss the Silver Dollar, *C. hemisphaerica,* a small, perfectly round plant whose closely overlapping green leaves always attract attention. Neither should one overlook the jewel-like St. Andrew's Cross, *C. triebneri,* whose pale yellow-green leaves form a perfect cross, beautifully flushed and dotted with red in winter. Then, too, there are several small species with flat, wedge-shaped leaves so closely packed together that they seem laminated, such as the difficult but amazing Pyramid Crassula, *C. pyramidalis,* and the very easy, mosslike Elephant Grass, *C. lycopodioides.* And, finally, one must include the strange Rattlesnake Crassula, *C. teres,* whose incurved leaves form a tightly packed column like the overlapping plates in a rattlesnake's rattle, but are topped with a tuft of wonderfully fragrant white blossoms.

Of course no brief list can do justice to the hundreds of splendid and familiar plants this genus contains. What better ground cover or basket plants could one find than the delightful winter- and spring-blooming *C. lactea* and *C. multicava?* What nicer pot plants than the chubby white Silver Beads, *C. deltoidea,* or the ruddy *C. justi-corderoyi?* What greater novelty than the densely bearded *C. barbata,* whose tiny globular form and dense hairs make it look so much like a little woolly cactus? The list is endless.

In marked contrast to the varied and interesting crassulas, plants in the genus *Rochea* are neither very succulent nor striking but they do have magnificent flowers. The thin, closely packed leaves and erect stems form small, shrubby plants a foot or two high that are topped with large clusters of outstandingly beautiful flowers ranging from white through yellow, pink, and red. One species with scarlet flowers, *R. coccinea,* is perhaps the best known of all flowering succulents as it has been grown extensively by florists for the house-plant trade.

Seeds or stem cuttings are started in spring, and the plants

OTHER SUCCULENT FAMILIES

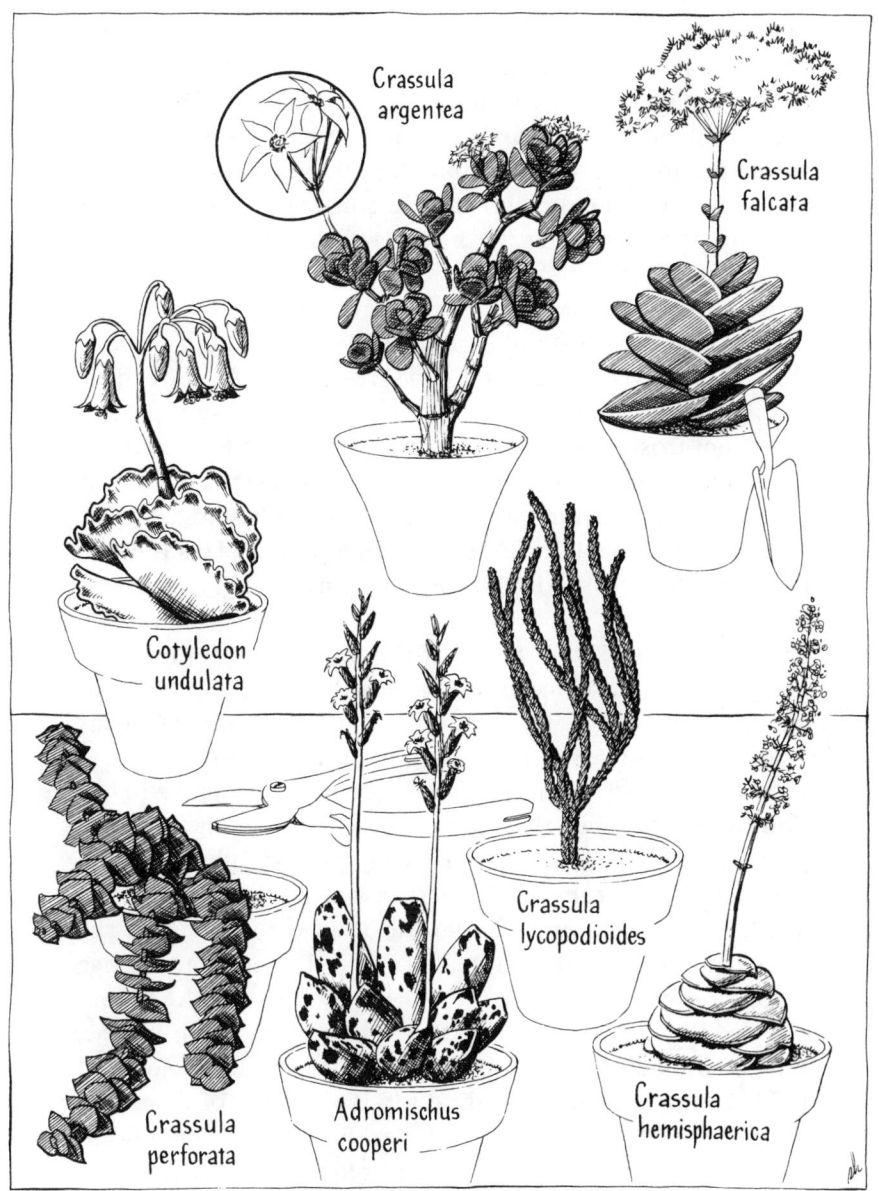

THE CRASSULA FAMILY

are kept bushy by pinching and moving up to a slightly larger pot once in summer and again in early fall. They are kept cool and slightly moist through the winter, but given ample heat, sunlight, food, and water as growth begins again in spring to force the long and abundant flowering in early summer. Although the rocheas require considerable handling to develop specimen plants, their stunning flowers are well worth the effort.

Actually most members of the Crassula tribe are rugged plants, able to withstand a great deal of abuse and neglect. But all species, especially the low-growing kinds, show their best form and color when given a well-drained soil, protection from frost, moderate watering, and ample light and air. With such treatment many of the larger species will soon outgrow their accommodations and have to be moved on or replaced with younger plants from time to time. This is easily accomplished by seed in spring or stem cuttings at almost any time.

The Echeveria Tribe. Some of the most beautiful leaf succulents in the world are found in this third tribe of the Crassula family. They are contained in the important genus *Echeveria* (ek-e-vee'-ree-ah) and in three or four closely related genera—all relatively tender rosette plants native to our Southwest, Mexico, Central and northern South America. Some are tiny, stemless, clustering plants; others, many-branched low shrubs; still others, a single large rosette atop a heavy stem. But more important than their forms are the amazing colors and textures of their leaves. They range through every shade of green, variously tinted with red and purple; through frosty white, with highlights of pink, rose, blue, and amethyst; into wonderful hairy species as soft and richly colored as velvet. And, to top it all, many of them produce graceful, long-lasting tubular flowers in magnificent spikes of bright yellow, orange, and red. It is no wonder they are so widely grown and so well loved.

In the eighty or more species of the genus *Echeveria* we can find a wide selection of really choice plants for any home or garden. Among the very small echeverias one should not miss *E. amoena, E. microcalyx,* or *E. expatriata,* whose close rosettes and tiny pinkish flowers are delightful miniatures. But it is in the medium-sized species, with rosettes three or four inches in diameter, that we find the greatest number of familiar plants. Here are those well-known summer-bedding plants grown in parks the world over, *E. secunda* and *E. glauca,* popularly called Hen and Chickens because they form a circle of smaller rosettes around each mother plant. And here too are the alabaster-white rosettes of *E. elegans;* the lovely Painted Lady, *E. derenbergii,* whose pale green leaves are tipped bright red; the silver-blue rosettes of *E. peacockii;* and that wonderful winter bloomer *E. carnicolor,* with its narrow flesh-colored leaves and brilliant orange-red flowers.

In this group we might also mention those beautiful hairy-leaved species such as the Mexican Firecracker, *E. setosa,* whose short green rosettes are completely covered with glistening white hairs and topped with vivid red and yellow flowers. And we must not overlook the finest of them all—the velvety Plush Plant, *E. pulvinata,* with its brown felted stems and green leaves tipped red; or that other shrubby species so much like it, the silvery-white Chenille Plant, *E. leucotricha.* Neither must we forget that other little bushy species with velvety leaves and the biggest, brightest red flowers of them all, *E. harmsii.*

But the echeverias really reach their greatest beauty in the large-growing species, those huge, loose, cabbage-like rosettes which reach a foot or more in diameter on heavy stems. And of these the finest, the most typical, is *E. gibbiflora.* In the variety *metallica* the large, broad leaves are a soft pinkish bronze touched with white and red along the margins. A perfect specimen two or three feet high with tall, branched flower spikes crowded with a profusion of scarlet flowers is an unforgettable sight. The variety *carunculata* has somewhat narrower leaves with strange blister-like growths on their upper surfaces. And the variety *crispata* is highly prized for its wavy, crinkled leaf margins. Two other large species, somewhat different from *E. gibbiflora* and its varieties, but almost as much admired, are *E. crenulata,* with wavy, red-margined leaves, and *E. hoveyi,* with long, narrow, gray-green leaves beautifully variegated with pink and cream stripes.

There are scores of other fine echeveria species, varieties, and hybrids too numerous to mention. They all make splendid potted plants indoors or out—on patios, porches, terraces, and lanais. And as landscape plants they are simply indispensable for wall plantings and ground covers, rock gardens and formal beds. Indeed, the beginner will find the echeverias and their relatives among the easiest, most useful of all succulents.

Of the several genera related to the echeverias the genus *Dudleya* (dud'-lee-ah) is the largest and perhaps the least known. It contains about eighty species, all native to California and that part of Mexico called Lower California. The dudleyas are rosette plants with long, tapering, persistent leaves which form single or clustered rosettes ranging in color from pale green to snowy white. Their white, yellow, or reddish flowers are not especially interesting, but the spectacular white foliage of several species makes them outstanding plants in any collection.

Probably the best known of the snowy dudleyas is the Chalk Lettuce, *D. pulverulenta,* which forms an eighteen-inch rosette of intensely white leaves. *D. ingens* and *D. brittonii* are other large species with the same handsome foliage. And among the smaller species *D. candida* and *D. farinosa* are wonderful little white clustering plants. All these dudleyas are of the easiest culture and, strangely enough, seem to grow better in pots than in the open ground.

Quite unlike the spectacular dudleyas, the tiny Mexican genus *Urbinia* (ur-bin'-ee-ah) contains only a handful of modest little plants. All of them have thick, sharply pointed leaves held in a close rosette and slender, moderately attractive flower spikes. The best-known species is *U. agavoides*, whose smooth, shiny, fat green leaves stand a little erect like its namesake, the agaves. It makes an interesting small potted plant, especially in its freakish cristate form. Other good species, though somewhat similar, are *U. corderoyi* and the brown-spotted *U. purpusii*.

Of far greater value to the collector is the attractive genus *Pachyphytum* (pa-kif'-i-tum), whose thick, rounded leaves attached to stout, erect stems are perhaps the most exquisitely shaped and colored in the whole Echeveria tribe. These are beautiful plants, with pearl-toned leaves and stunning bell-shaped flowers that are a "must" for any collection. Among the eight or nine species in the genus we might select *P. compactum* for its short, cylindrical, blue-gray leaves and subtly colored blossoms; or *P. bracteosum*, with its thick gray-white leaves and bright red spring flowers. But the finest of them all is *P. oviferum*, whose thick, fleshy, egg-shaped leaves are like smooth Moonstones softly flushed with lavender pink, hence its popular name.

It is not surprising that hybridists have tried to extend the rare colors and forms of these pachyphytums to other members of the tribe. To this end they have crossed the echeverias with the pachyphytums to produce a race of hybrids called *Pachyveria* (pak-i-vee'-ree-ah). These are all very popular plants because they partake something of both their parents. Here the rosette form of the echeverias and the plump, richly colored leaves of the pachyphytums are combined in such hybrids as *Pachyveria glauca*, whose thick rosettes are powdered and mottled blue gray; *P. scheideckeri*, with fine whitish-green rosettes; and that wonderful crested variety, *P. clavifolia cristata*.

Most members of the Echeveria tribe are exceptionally easy and rugged plants, requiring only the simplest culture. While they will tolerate almost any soil, they grow best when given a fairly rich humus mixture with good drainage and ample water. Free ventilation and light indoors will prevent the plants becoming weak or drawn, and summering out of doors will ensure good form and foliage. Species with smooth leaves do best in full sun; those with hairy leaves prefer some shade. Although a few species such as the common Hen and Chickens can survive below-zero temperatures, most members of the Echeveria tribe are fairly tender to frost and should be protected from freezing in winter. Propagation is easily accomplished with offsets formed by clustering species; stem cuttings of shrubby species; leaf cuttings of certain small species such as *Echeveria amoena;* or plantlets formed on the flower stalks of several large species, as *E. gibbiflora.* Seeds are virtually useless for propagating any particular species, because unless pollination is carefully controlled members of this tribe hybridize freely among themselves, producing innumerable variants.

The Kalanchoe Tribe. Although they comprise a relatively small group of plants in cultivation, with fairly distinct characteristics, members of this fourth tribe of the Crassula family are perhaps the most confused in nomenclature. Actually there are three distinct genera in this tribe: the genus *Kalanchoe* (kal-an-koh'-ee), which is characterized by erect flowers; the genus *Bryophyllum* (bry-oh-fi'-lum), with pendent flowers and leaves that often produce plantlets along their margins; and the genus *Kitchingia* (ki-ching'-ee-ah), whose pendent flowers resemble the bryophyllums, but can be differentiated by having anthers which are attached to the upper part of the flower petals and wide-spreading ovaries. In botanical literature, however, these three generic names have been used almost interchangeably, and now one may find them all simply listed as *Kalanchoe.*

OTHER SUCCULENT FAMILIES

Actually the genus *Kalanchoe* is by far the largest in the tribe, with over two hundred species scattered over Africa, India, China, Malaysia, Madagascar, and even tropical America. The kalanchoes are generally small shrubby plants, usually a foot or two in height, with succulent opposite leaves. Several species produce a profusion of small brightly colored winter flowers that have long been prized as house plants for the Christmas season. Outstanding among these are the ever popular scarlet *K. blossfeldiana* and *K. flammea,* the fragrant pink *K. carnea,* and a host of florists' varieties, with flowers ranging from white and yellow through deep purple.

Of several species grown primarily for their interesting foliage none is more popular than the Panda Plant, *K. tomentosa,* whose silvery plush leaves stained rich red brown at the margins are loved the world over. Equally interesting are the heavily spotted gray-green leaves of the Pen Wiper Plant, *K. marmorata;* and the huge, treelike Velvet Elephant Ear, *K. beharensis.* This largest member of the Kalanchoe tribe has thick, velvety, silver-brown triangular leaves up to eighteen inches across, and has recently found great favor in landscaping with other bold tropical-foliage plants. Although *Kalanchoe beharensis* is sometimes grown under the name *Kitchingia mandrakensis,* the seven or eight species of kitchingia native to Madagascar are seldom met with in cultivation.

Unlike the rare kitchingias, the prolific bryophyllums are in evidence everywhere succulents are grown. Most of the twenty or more species native to Madagascar, like the ubiquitous *B. pinnatum,* have encircled the globe because of their curious habit of bearing hundreds of tiny plantlets along their leaf margins which fall to earth ready to grow. Indeed, they reproduce themselves so easily that many gardeners have come to regard them as weeds. But despite this embarrassing productivity few succulents are more interesting in reproduction, vigorous in growth, or colorful in flower. A few bryophyllums are a "must" in any collection, for their great clusters of pendent, bell-shaped flowers are unique among all succulents.

Of the shrubby, sprouting-leaf species none is more curious than the Air Plant, *B. tubiflorum,* whose tubular green and brown leaves bear innumerable plantlets at their tips and a wealth of orange-red flowers in winter. Equally prolific and beautiful are the species *B. crenatum* and *B. fedtschenkoi,* which have small, rounded, frosty-green leaves suffused pinkish red, and red flowers in winter. A very showy species with large arrow-shaped leaves, green spotted brown, is *B. daigremontianum,* whose numerous plantlets and yellow and pink winter flowers have made it extremely popular.

Aside from these sprouting-leaf species one must not overlook two bryophyllums which are noted for their strong climbing and trailing habit. *B. scandens* is a very interesting climber whose curious foliage and flowers can only be described as "mouse-colored"; and *B. uniflorum,* a wonderful hanging-basket plant with small green leaves and dainty red spring blossoms that have been aptly dubbed Chinese Lanterns.

All members of the Kalanchoe tribe are easily grown and propagated, with no special requirements except protection from frost in winter. They are excellent pot plants indoors, where their bright winter flowers and interesting foliage are greatly appreciated. As house plants they do best in full sunlight, but when planted out of doors they seem to prefer light shade at least part of the day. The florists' kalanchoes are usually treated as annuals and propagated for winter bloom by seed sown in early spring. Other species are propagated by stem cuttings, leaf cuttings, or by plantlets formed on the leaf margins, as in the genus *Bryophyllum.*

The Sedum Tribe. The genus *Sedum* (see'-dum), which dominates the fifth tribe of the Crassula family, is native to

OTHER SUCCULENT FAMILIES

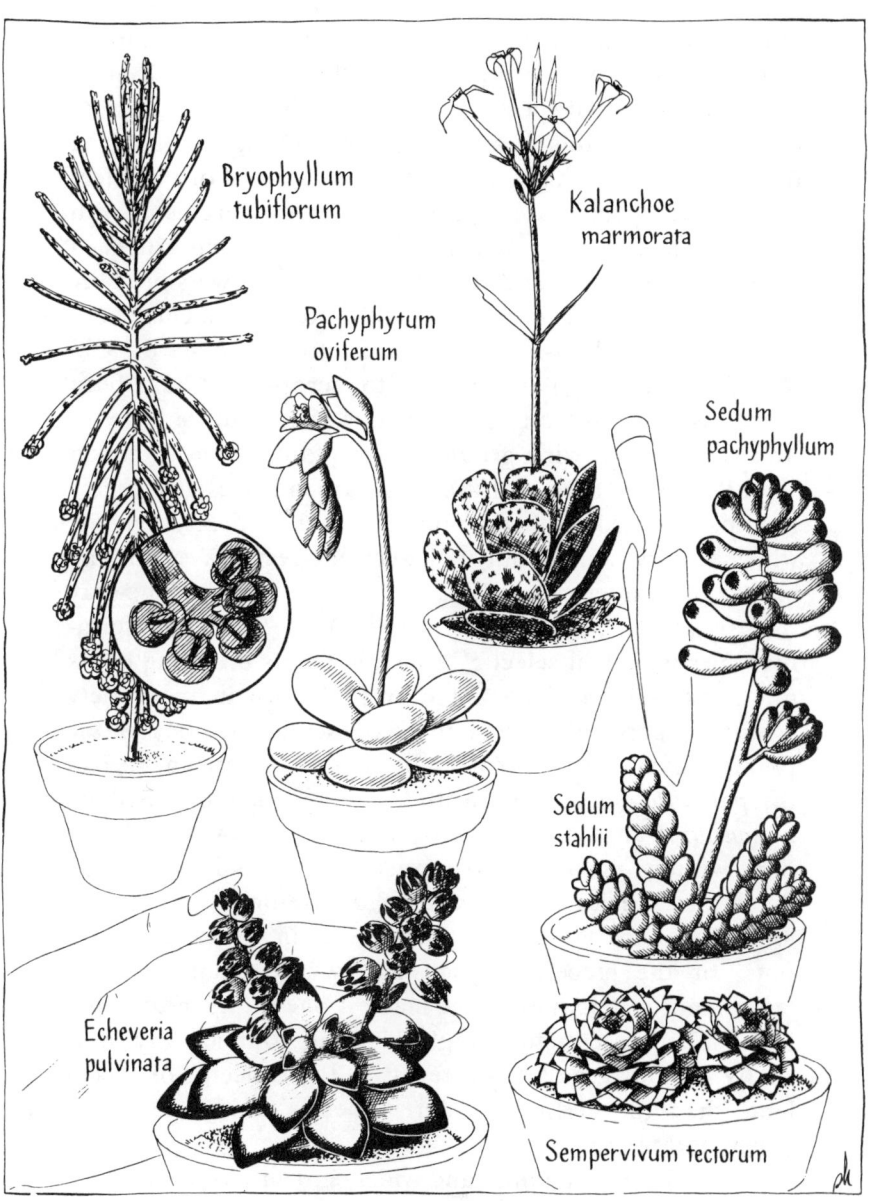

THE CRASSULA FAMILY

almost every part of the Northern Hemisphere and mountainous regions as far south as the Philippines. With more than three hundred species, it presents a bewildering variety of forms—from tiny beadlike plants forming mats only a fraction of an inch high to sprawling shrubs two or three feet tall. Some species are deciduous, some evergreen—with fleshy, succulent leaves arranged alternately, opposite each other, or in whorls—and the small, starlike flowers of many kinds are brightly colored and displayed in large clusters.

Perhaps the best-known sedums are those hardy Old World species, popularly called Stonecrops, that have been grown as rock-garden and wall plants for centuries. Here we find such low-growing ground-cover plants as the common Wall Pepper, *S. acre,* with tiny pale green leaves and yellow blooms crowded on fast-creeping branches; *S. sexangulare,* which is very similar but with darker green leaves turning bronze in winter; and, best of all, the dainty blue-gray *S. dasyphyllum,* with pinkish flowers. Of the larger mat-forming types we might select *S. reflexum* for its drooping heads of yellow flowers and strange crested form in the variety *cristatum,* popularly called the Cockscomb Sedum; or the plump silvery rosettes of that superb American species *S. spathulifolium;* or the brilliant Dragon's Blood Sedum, *S. spurium* var. *coccineum,* with its crimson flowers and brilliant winter foliage. And we must not overlook such hardy deciduous species as *S. spectabile,* whose broad gray leaves and showy pink flowers are unsurpassed in flower borders or pots; or the graceful *S. sieboldii,* whose dainty notched leaves and trailing habit have made it one of the most popular of all succulents for hanging baskets. But actually these hardy sedums are of less interest to the collector of succulents than the fleshier, tenderer species which are native chiefly to Mexico.

One of the most familiar and widely grown succulents in the world is the shrubby Mexican species *S. praealtum,* whose shiny, green, spoon-shaped leaves and bright yellow summer flowers are borne on a tough, bushy plant two or three feet high and as wide. Two other popular shrubby species of much more refined habit are the foot-high *S. treleasei,* with thick blue-white leaves and yellow flowers; and the choice Golden Sedum, *S. adolphi,* whose handsome yellow leaves and white flowers are a valuable addition to any collection.

Another distinct group of tender, shrubby sedums are those species with sausage-shaped leaves. Here we find the foot-high *S. pachyphyllum,* with dainty gray-green leaves tipped red, and yellow spring flowers; *S. allantoides,* which looks very much like it but has snowy-white leaves and blossoms; *S. guatemalense,* a miniature version of both, whose shiny green leaves turn bright red in the sun, giving it the popular name Christmas Cheer; and the well-known Boston Bean, *S. stahlii,* a low-growing species with very fat round leaves that turn red brown in the sun. In this group we must also mention the recently discovered *S. morganianum,* an outstanding hanging-basket plant whose pendent branches, thick with silvery leaves, often reach three feet in length, giving it the apt name Burro's Tail.

There is also a group of small, bushy Mexican sedums with flatter, thinner leaves, such as the closely related *S. compressum* and *S. palmeri,* whose slender, sprawling stems bear rosettes of loosely arranged, rounded whitish leaves and orange-yellow flowers in spring. Two other low-growing, mat-forming species are *S. amecamecanum,* with yellow-green leaves and pale yellow flowers, and *S. moranense,* with very small triangular leaves and white flowers. And to complete the list we must include that relatively tender Algerian species *S. multiceps,* whose small erect branches with close-tufted rosettes of tiny dark green leaves look for all the world like miniature pine trees.

Certainly no brief summary such as this can hope to do justice to the many hundreds of fine sedums available to every collector of succulents. As ground covers or wall plantings, in rockeries or borders, in pots or dish gardens, the sedums are among the easiest, most satisfactory of all succulents to grow. Every collection should include some of the species mentioned here, and as many more as space and interest will allow.

There is only one other important member in the Sedum tribe, the genus *Graptopetalum* (grap-toh-pet'-a-lum). Although the graptopetalums consist of only seven or eight species, all native to our Southwest and Mexico, they have endured a long history of changing names, synonyms, and tribes. But for once the confusion of names is understandable, for the graptopetalums really look more like echeverias and pachyphytums than sedums. They are all wonderful rosette plants with thick, subtly colored and tinted leaves; and only their wide-spreading flower petals, spotted and streaked with reddish brown, mark them as members of the Sedum tribe.

There are two very popular species of graptopetalum which should be included in every succulent collection. The first is the Amethyst Plant, *G. amethystinum,* which so nearly resembles *Pachyphytum bracteosum* that it is often mistakenly called a pachyphytum too. It is a handsome plant, eight or ten inches high, forming rosettes of thick, oval, amethyst-purple leaves tinted with highlights of pink and blue. The second species is the universally popular Ghost Plant, *G. paraguayense,* which has innumerable aliases such as *Graptopetalum* or *Byrnesia* or *Echeveria weinbergii.* It gets its single popular name, however, from the soft gray-green color of its flat, pointed leaves, which are touched with highlights of pink, red, and purple, and seem to glow softly at dusk. But despite its delicate appearance this graptopetalum, as most of the other species, will stand an amazing amount of hardship and neglect. Perhaps that is why it is one of the most widely grown and well-loved succulents we have today.

This combination of unbelievable toughness and delicate beauty is a common trait of all the Sedum tribe. No other succulents seem to grow and propagate quite so easily. Only the tender Mexican and Mediterranean species require occasional shading in summer or protection from frost; the others are hardy and self-sufficient almost anywhere the year round. All species are quickly and easily propagated either by leaf or stem cuttings, or seeds or divisions.

The Sempervivum Tribe. The sixth and last tribe of the Crassula family, like the fifth, contains two distinct groups of succulent plants—one hardy, the other tender. The hardy members are contained in the well-known genus of European alpine plants called *Sempervivum* (sem-per-vy'-vum), the tender ones in several African genera related to it. They are all rosette plants, somewhat reminiscent of the echeverias, yet distinct in the shape and texture of their leaves, their growing habits, and blooms.

The genus *Sempervivum* consists of about twenty-five species of small, stemless, many-leaved rosettes native to the mountains of Central and Southern Europe. Although the individual plants are only one fourth inch to six inches in diameter, they produce innumerable offsets from their leaf axils which form clusters and eventually great mats, sometimes a yard or more in diameter. The starry pink, white, yellow, or purple flowers are borne in dense heads each summer, after which the flowering rosettes die. Although these hardy sempervivums, or Houseleeks, as they are popularly called, are perhaps of greater interest to the collector of rock-garden and alpine plants, they have much to offer the succulent enthusiast as well. In rock and wall gardens, borders and patterned beds, pots and dish gardens, no other succulents—except perhaps the sedums—can equal them for easy culture and rugged beauty.

Of the smaller species no collection can afford to miss the exquisite Cobweb Houseleek, *S. arachnoideum,* whose half-inch rosettes are densely covered with cobweb-like white hairs; or the slightly larger, darker green species, *S. montanum,* noted for its bright purple flowers. Of the larger sempervivums none is more popular or widely grown than the Common Houseleek, *S. tectorum* var. *calcareum,* whose three-inch, gray-green rosettes have a pronounced brown tip on each leaf; or the huge six-inch rosettes of *S. calcaratum,* beautifully shaded and tinted with crimson and purple highlights. The list is really endless, for the sempervivums hybridize readily and the number of fine varieties now available to collectors probably runs into the thousands.

Closely related to these hardy European sempervivums are a group of tender species native to North Africa and the Canary, Cape Verde, and Madeira Islands. They belong to four genera, of which the largest and most important is the genus *Aeonium* (ee-oh'-ni-um). The aeoniums are generally small, shrubby plants with woody stems topped with flat or saucer-shaped rosettes of attractive succulent leaves. Their flowers are freely produced in late winter or early spring in huge pyramidal clusters of bright yellow, white, pink, or red; and, like most members of the Sempervivum tribe, this flowering usually signals the death of the plants unless they have produced other branches or offshoots to continue growth.

Perhaps the best known of all aeoniums is the bushy *A. arboreum,* which makes an erect three-foot shrub topped with numerous light green rosettes and bright yellow flowers. It is one of the commonest and most popular succulents out of doors in mild climates, and particularly striking in the variety *atropurpureum,* with bronze-red leaves that turn almost black in the sun. *A. haworthii,* with white flowers and blue-green leaves edged in red, and *A. decorum,* with bright coppery-red leaves and pink flowers, are two other shrubby species that are scarcely half as large but equally well liked as potted plants indoors or out.

Other aeonium species have very short stems and either form small clumps or bear a single large rosette at their tip. *A. caespitosum* is a fine example of the clump-forming type. Its narrow green leaves, striped with red and bearing white hairs along their margins, form cushions of dense rosettes that close up like bulbs during their summer resting period. Of the single rosette forms none is more curious than *A. tabulaeforme,* which makes an absolutely flat rosette a foot or more in diameter consisting of hundreds of closely imbricated green leaves. Equally stunning is the huge *A. canariense,* whose broad, spoon-shaped leaves are covered with velvety white hairs and form a single rosette nearly two feet in diameter. But the finest of them all is the magnificent *A. nobile,* whose broad, fleshy, olive-green leaves form a rosette twenty inches across topped by an immense head of coppery scarlet flowers.

Of the other tender African genera belonging to the Sempervivum tribe only one is at all common in succulent collections, the genus *Greenovia* (gree-no'-vee-ah). It consists of four species, all native to mountainous regions of the Canary Islands and all closely related to the aeoniums. They are neat little clustering rosette plants with thin, spoon-shaped, waxy green leaves and bright yellow spring flowers. Ordinarily they would not excite much attention, but they have one curious habit that makes them irresistible. During their resting period in the hot summer months they pull up their leaves to form a tight cylinder which looks for all the world like a half-open rosebud, hence their popular name, Green Rosebuds. The two most widely grown species are *G. aurea,* with blue-green clustered rosettes up to five inches in diameter; and *G. dodrentalis,* with much smaller gray-green rosettes that form dense, cushion-like mats.

All members of the Sempervivum tribe are of the easiest culture, requiring only the minimum care given any succulents. The tender aeoniums and greenovias must, of course, be protected from frost in winter; but the hardy sempervivums need no protection except perhaps a thin covering of leaves or litter in the coldest areas. Unfortunately the propagation of some of these plants is complicated by the fact that they die after flowering. While most species produce new branches or offsets to continue growth and are as easily propagated by cuttings or divisions as any succulents, those that have only a single stem and produce no offsets, as *Aeonium nobile* and *tabulaeforme,* must usually be propagated by seed. This curious fact accounts for the relative rarity of some of the largest and finest species in this tribe.

The Daisy Family—The *Compositae*

While some plant families, like the Cactus and Crassula, have become almost wholly succulent in the process of evolution, others like the vast Daisy, or Composite, family have developed surprisingly few succulent members. Actually the succulent relatives of our sunflowers, daisies, and thistles are found in only three or four closely related genera, the most important of which is the genus *Kleinia* (kly'-ni-ah).

The kleinias are generally small succulent shrubs or trailing plants with fleshy stems and leaves and thistlelike flowers, all native to North and South Africa, the Canary Islands, and the East Indies. Perhaps the best-known species is the popular Candle Plant, *K. articulata,* whose thick, jointed, waxy green stems form an erect two-foot shrub bearing bluish leaves and white flowers during the winter growing season. Two other species with very similar growth habits are *K. anteuphorbium,* which makes a five-foot shrub with somewhat thinner stems, and *K. neriifolia,* which forms very thick stems up to ten feet high crowned with a rosette of leaves that disappear at the first sign of drought. In this same group we might also include the curious Inchworm Plant, *K. pendula,* a clustering dwarf whose thick, naked stems loop up and down as they go forward across the ground and finally bear large flower heads that look like scarlet carnations.

Quite distinct from these thick-stemmed shrubby species which shed their leaves after the growing season are a number of low, trailing plants with fleshy, persistent leaves. Probably the most popular of these is the handsome *K. repens,* whose brilliant, blue-green, cylindrical leaves have been aptly named Blue Chalk Sticks. Very similar but larger in all ways are *K. ficoides* and *K. mandraliscae,* and very much smaller in all respects is that excellent hanging-basket plant *K. radicans.* But the finest of all these trailing kleinias is the snowy-white *K. tomentosa,* whose soft, cocoon-like, felted leaves are admired the world over.

The genus *Senecio* (se-nee'-shi-oh) is so similar in most respects to the genus *Kleinia* that the two have been combined and separated repeatedly in botanical literature. Actually there are some minor differences in the thistlelike flowers of these two genera, and popular usage now seems to favor keeping them apart. The senecios are native to Cape Province and Southwest Africa, and although they comprise a relatively large group of succulent herbs, shrubs, and vines, only two species are common in amateur collections. *Senecio scaposus,* with its rosettes of slender, six-inch, white felted leaves, is an exceptionally handsome plant in any collection. And the curious Candy Stick, *S. stapeliiformis,* is as much admired for its thick, many-angled stems as for its bright red summer flowers.

Because they have typical daisy flowers, plants in the genus *Othonna* (oh-thon'-ah) are perhaps the most easily recognized succulent members of the Daisy family. Although there are many species of othonna in South Africa, only one is commonly grown by amateurs, *O. crassifolia.* It is difficult to imagine a more beautiful hanging-basket or ground-cover plant than this dainty trailer. It is prized not only for its myriad bright yellow flowers displayed the year round, but for its tiny fresh-green leaves that have been aptly dubbed Little Pickles.

All these succulent members of the Daisy family are tender and must be planted in a well-drained soil, given careful watering and protection from frost. Careful watering is perhaps most important as these plants are very susceptible to rot during their resting period. Those thick-stemmed species which renew their leaves annually, like *Kleinia articulata,* usually rest in summer after their leaves have fallen; species with persistent leaves, like *Kleinia tomentosa,* usually rest during the winter. Water must therefore be applied sparingly during these dormant periods. While most members of this family may be raised from seed, the preferred method of propagation is by stem cuttings, which root very easily throughout the growing season.

The Euphorbia Family—The *Euphorbiaceae*

Of the two hundred or more genera in the immense family *Euphorbiaceae* (eu-four-bi-ay'-see-ee) only one is of great interest to succulent collectors, the genus *Euphorbia* (eu-four'-bi-ah). With more than a thousand species scattered over the entire world, it contains most of the succulent plants in the family. But it must be remembered that not all the euphorbias are succulent. Many are common weeds in our fields and byways; others, familiar annuals, like the Mexican Fire Plant, *E. heterophylla;* or Snow on the Mountain, *E. marginata;* still others, perennial shrubs or trees, like the popular Christmas Poinsettia, *E. pulcherrima.*

It is interesting to note that almost all the euphorbias of Europe and America are "normal" plants, while those of southern Asia and Africa are succulents. Thus the best known of all euphorbias, the Crown of Thorns, *E. splendens,* is a slender, spiny shrub from Madagascar whose brown half-woody branches bear a few leaves at their tips and clusters of flowers with bright scarlet bracts from spring till fall. Still more clearly succulent are the shrubby species *E. dregeana* and *E. mauritanica* from South Africa, whose slender, wandlike stems bear no spines, only transient leaflets, and often form

OTHER SUCCULENT FAMILIES

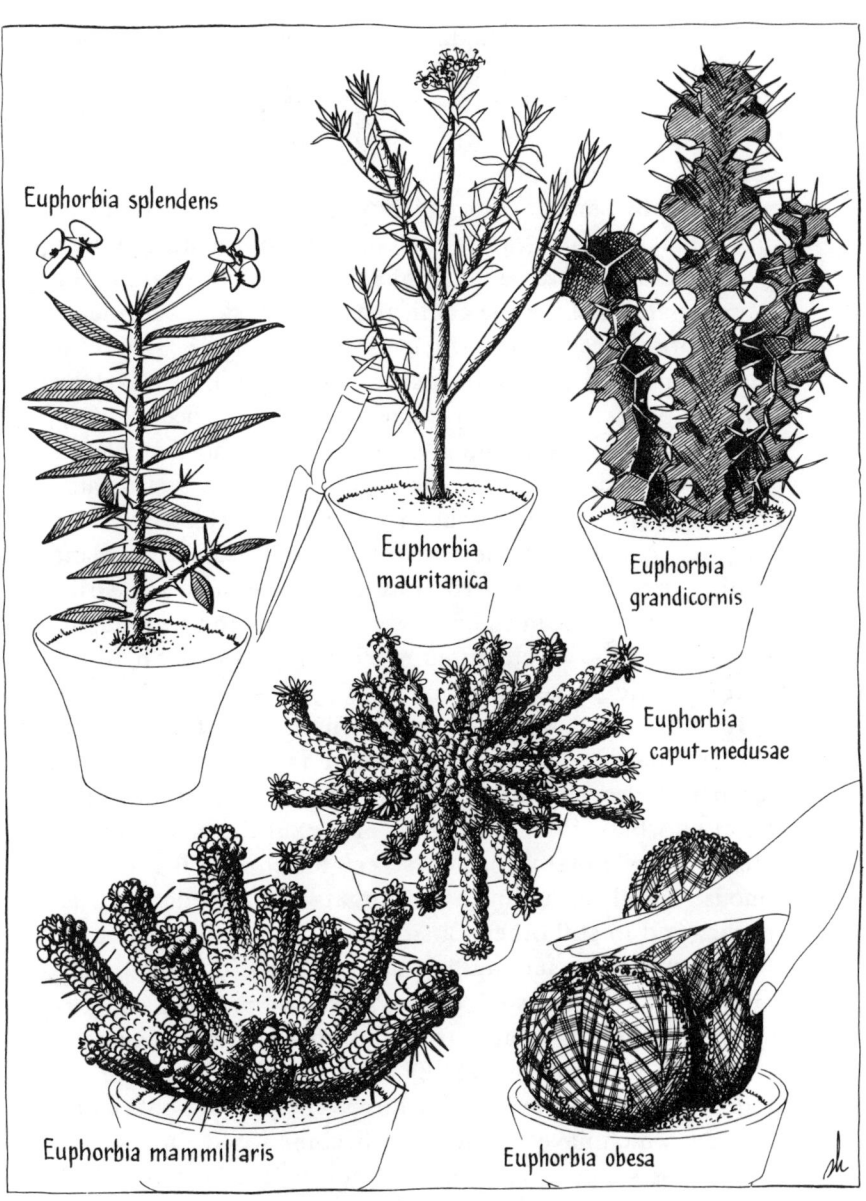

THE EUPHORBIA FAMILY

intricate crests much sought after by collectors. And when we reach those highly succulent, cactus-like euphorbias that range from India and southern Arabia through all of Africa to the Cape Province, we suddenly realize the immense wealth at our disposal.

It is really amazing to see how closely these succulent euphorbias resemble cacti. Indeed, many of them have been given cactus names, as *E. opuntioides, E. cereiformis,* or *E. mammillaris.* Like the cacti, they are all stem succulents with more or less transient leaves. They range in size from tiny compressed plants an inch or two high, much like the Living Rocks, to great columnar and treelike species rising sixty feet or more resembling the giant Torch and Candelabra Cacti. This uncanny resemblance is one of the classic examples of parallel development in the plant world. For under the same pressures of necessity two totally different plant families in widely separated continents have taken on strikingly similar forms in the process of adaptation to drought. In every way the succulent euphorbias are to the Old World what cacti are to the New.

But while the novice may be confused at first by the outward similarities of these two plant families, there are a number of clear-cut differences which will help him identify the euphorbias. First, all euphorbias exude a milky sap, or latex, which in many species is very bitter, burning, or poisonous; in others, useful as a purgative or emetic, such as ipecac; and in still others, a source of low-grade rubber. In the Cactus family such milky sap is a rarity, occurring only among certain species of *Mammillaria.* Second, the euphorbias do not produce spines from cushion-like growth centers, or areoles, along the stems like cacti, but directly out of the stem itself. These spines are of three types: side shoots along the stem which have aborted and become woody and sharp; stipules, or small leaflike appendages, at the base of a leaf stalk which have hardened, forming pairs of spines; or flower stems which have become woody and remained on the plant to give protection. Third, the euphorbias have a curious and complicated inflorescence utterly unlike the simple and showy cactus bloom. The euphorbia blossom is actually a cluster of flowers called a cyathium (sy-ath'-ee-um). It consists of a cup, formed by the fusion of several bracts, within which are contained several diminutive male flowers and a single female flower. In some species the male and female flowers occupy separate cyathia or even grow on separate plants. Unfortunately these delightfully intricate blooms are usually inconspicuous, as the bracts are small, dull green or yellow; but occasionally they may be large and brilliantly colored, as in the Crown of Thorns, *E. splendens,* or the Poinsettia, where the whole inflorescence looks like a single flower. And, finally, the fruit of the euphorbias is usually a three-lobed capsule, each lobe with a single seed, and it bursts explosively when ripe.

It is obviously impossible to set down here all the hundreds of species, varieties, and forms of succulent euphorbias known to collectors. But it may help to survey briefly some of the more popular and interesting kinds for the beginner.

Of the dwarf species the most interesting are those which have a strong main stem buried in the soil from which springs a twisting, swirling head of spineless, snaky branches a foot or more in length. Perhaps the most popular of these is the Snake's Head Euphorbia, *E. caput-medusae,* whose writhing, snakelike branches recall the serpent hair of Medusa in Greek mythology. Somewhat similar and equally popular are *E. bergeri* and *E. inermis.*

Another group of dwarf euphorbias, somewhat like the Living Rock and Star Cacti in appearance, is the perfectly globular species. Here we find the tiny round branches of *E. globosa,* which grow in large mats on the surface of the soil and are about the size of marbles. And here too is the very popular *E. obesa,* a perfectly hard, rounded, spineless plant about eight inches in height whose angled ribs, curiously striped and shaded, have won for it the descriptive name Basket Ball Euphorbia. Very similar and equally popular are *E. meloformis* and *E. valida,* but they develop very stout, branched flower stalks which become woody after flowering and persist. All these species, except *E. globosa,* are dioecious (dy-ee'-shus), that is, their male and female flowers are borne on separate plants.

Even more cactus-like in appearance are a number of low cylindrical species led off by the ever popular Corn Cob Euphorbia, *E. mammillaris.* The eight-inch branches of this curious plant form clusters that look for all the world like spiny green corn cobs. No less deserving of its name is *E. horrida,* whose deeply grooved and ribbed stems display a fierce array of thorns that any Barrel Cactus might envy. And one other cylindrical species commands our interest, *E. bupleurifolia.* For a greater part of the year this euphorbia looks like a small fir cone, because its thick stem is covered spirally with knobs which are old leaf bases; then in spring it produces a beautiful topknot of narrow leaves, and is transformed for a while into a perfect little pineapple, hence its popular name, Pineapple Euphorbia. A slender version of this plant is found in *E. clandestina,* whose very erect two-foot stems are affectionately called the Soldier.

The last and largest group of succulent euphorbias we must consider are those large shrubby or treelike species which have angled stems and prominent spines, generally held in pairs. While many of these are naturally useless to the collector because of their great size, uninteresting form, or vicious armor, there remain a large number of extremely attractive, slow-growing species that can be included as small plants in any collection.

Of the shrubby species one might select at random such fine plants as *E. pseudocactus* for the distinctive yellow-green markings on its stems; the Devil's Club, *E. cereiformis,* for its easy growth; *E. polygona* for handsome ribbed stems; or *E. coerulescens* for the beautiful blue-green color of its new branches. But the finest of them all is *E. grandicornis,* whose three-foot stems branching from the base are pinched off into short three-angled joints, each studded with very long paired spines that give it the popular name Cow's Horns.

Just as small plants of the giant Torch and Candelabra Cacti are useful and interesting in succulent collections, so young plants of the large treelike euphorbias may serve as an ideal background for the smaller types. Among them we can find such wonderfully interesting plants as *E. abyssinica,* whose deeply ribbed branches are curiously veined and whorled; *E. canariensis,* a very popular and elegant species with slender, erect branches; or the Elk's Horn Euphorbia, *E. lactea* var. *cristata,* whose crested, knobby branches are a worthy rival of the Peruvian Rock Cactus, *Cereus peruvianus* var. *monstrosus,* and as much sought after. But none of these has quite the charm of *E. hermentiana,* the Milk Tree, whose erect, angular, dark green branches are beautifully mottled with white and studded with red-brown spines and surprisingly persistent tiny green leaves. It grows and branches very freely making a fine specimen that is a "must" for every collection.

The euphorbias are not difficult to grow but, like most succulents, they must have ample sunshine and air, protection from frost, and careful watering. Winter is the usual growing season for most species in mild climates, but in colder areas the plants must be kept dormant during the winter by keeping them cool and relatively dry, as moisture and cold combined quickly induce rot. As warm weather approaches, the plants may be watered more freely to stimulate new growth, but once this is completed they should be rested, with very little water the remainder of the year.

Great care should be taken in handling euphorbias as they "bleed" very easily when damaged. This not only disfigures the plant, but the milky juice is often dangerously poisonous or caustic and may cause serious injuries if it reaches the eyes, the mouth, or an open cut.

Euphorbias with branching stems are easily propagated by cuttings at the start of the growing season. They are sometimes slow to root, however, unless the excess milk which coagulates at the cut end is washed off in water and the cutting set on a shelf to dry for a few days. Cuttings of lateral branches from *E. caput-medusae* and its relatives present a special problem, as they sometimes continue to grow in length and fail to form their characteristic head. To correct this the rooted cutting must be cut back again close to the ground, at which time it will produce new shoots showing the typical "caput" form.

Some species such as *E. meloformis* can be propagated by offsets; but others, like *E. obesa,* which make neither branches nor offsets, can be propagated only by seed. Actually most euphorbias are quickly and easily raised from seed, but care should be taken to isolate or bag the seeding plants to prevent chance hybridization, and to cover the explosive capsule with a small cloth or paper sack to catch the ripe seeds.

Occasionally euphorbias that are especially rare, delicate, or weakened from loss of roots or decay are propagated by grafting. Either a flat or cleft graft is used, and *E. mammillaris* or the heavier *E. cereiformis* serve as understocks. As with cuttings, the milky sap is best washed from the scion and scraped gently from the cut portion of the understock to insure a clean fit.

The Lily Family—The *Liliaceae*

It is not surprising that the vast Lily family, which has given us so many valuable plants, from onions and asparagus to tulips and lilies, should also provide us with a remarkable group of succulents. These are contained in three popular genera, all of them leaf succulents and all natives of Africa.

The Genus Aloe. Certainly the most important succulents in the Lily family are found in the genus *Aloe* (al'-oh), which is native principally to South Africa. The aloes are all leaf succulents: that is, their thick, fleshy, pointed leaves are arranged spirally to form short rosettes—either with or without a stem. This has caused some people to confuse them with the American agaves, or Century Plants. But while there is a superficial resemblance, the agaves belong to the Amaryllis family, and have tough, fibrous leaves quite distinct from the soft, pulpy leaves of the aloes. It is simply another case of parallel development, for the aloes are to the Eastern Hemisphere what the agaves are to the West.

Among the nearly two hundred species of aloes we can find tiny stemless plants only an inch or two high, climbing and trailing forms, huge clustering shrubs, and giant treelike specimens fifty feet high. However, the aloes are not prized for these interesting plants alone, but for their magnificent flowers.

From October to April the South African veldt is aflame with aloe blooms. They rise from the plants in simple "red-hot pokers" or in great branched candelabras bearing hundreds of brilliant orange, red, or yellow tubular blossoms. And wherever the aloes have become established they still keep their blooming season. It is spring and summer in South Africa, but fall and winter in the West—a time when we most need bright color in our homes and gardens.

Because of their handsome form and spectacular bloom the aloes have been popular plants in the Mediterranean area since the eighteenth century. Ornate containers with large specimen aloes have been traditional decorative pieces on balconies and terraces, and thousands of plants have escaped cultivation to become completely naturalized along the Riviera.

But actually aloes were known in Greek and Roman times,

for the "bitter aloes" of the ancients was the resinous juice of *A. perryi,* widely used as a laxative. And in more recent times the healing juices in the leaves of *A. vera* have been effective in curing X-ray burns. The demand for leaves during World War II exhausted the supply of plants in several botanical gardens.

It is probably for these medicinal uses that the first aloes were brought to the West by the Spaniards. We find old plants of *A. vera* and other species in several mission gardens. In Mexico, particularly Lower California, these have occasionally escaped into the surrounding countryside covering many acres.

The species of aloes now readily available to collectors may be divided into three convenient groups. First, the small aloes—which may be used as house plants in pots and dish gardens, or in the foreground or border of succulent beds. Second, the medium-sized aloes—which are best as tub plants in the patio and garden, or in the middle section of succulent plantings. And, third, the large aloes—which are suitable as tall background plants or, where climate permits, may be naturalized in the open with other drought-resistant shrubs and trees.

Of the small aloes *A. brevifolia* is a very prolific little plant forming clumps of thick, gray-green rosettes three or four inches in diameter topped with an eighteen-inch spike of pale red flowers. Very similar but with smaller, incurved, toothy leaves is the popular Crocodile Aloe, *A. globosa.* Another small species which makes a very distinct rosette, about six inches high and as much across, is *A. aristata.* Its numerous thin, incurving leaves are gray green dotted with white and tipped and margined with almost hairlike teeth, which give the plant its popular name—Lace Aloe. But the finest and strangest of all is *A. variegata.* It makes a foot-high triangular rosette of erect three-cornered leaves that are a rich, dark green heavily marbled and margined with white. From these it gets its common name, Partridge-Breast or Tiger Aloe. In addition to these naturally small species young seedlings of even the large aloes, such as *A. ferox* and *A. marlothii,* may be used in pots and dish gardens, where they can be kept for some time without becoming too large.

Among the medium-sized species *A. striata* is a "must" for every collection. The broad, spineless, gray-green leaves of this aloe, bordered red along the margins, form a rosette about two feet in diameter. Out of this handsome plant rises a candelabra-like stem bearing hundreds of dazzling coral-orange flowers which give this plant its popular name—Coral Aloe. In marked contrast the bold, foot-wide rosettes of the Mitre Aloe, *A. mitriformis,* are formed of thick, triangular, bright green leaves edged with yellow teeth. These rosettes often rise in clustered sprawling columns four feet high and are topped with red flowers. Very nearly the same plant, only scaled down by half, is the popular Gold-spined Aloe, *A. nobilis.* But the greatest novelty in this group of medium-sized aloes is *A. ciliaris,* a truly climbing, sprawling species with pencil-thin stems sometimes ten feet long, bearing relatively small, thin, soft green leaves. Its masses of tiny red-orange flowers on short spikes have won for it the apt name Firecracker Aloe. In mild climates it makes an excellent ground cover on dry banks and walls.

Perhaps the most widely planted species of the larger aloes is *A. arborescens.* It forms a huge, shrubby plant ten feet high and ten feet wide that is aflame in midwinter with spires of bright "red-hot poker" blooms. Almost equally popular is *A. africana,* a fine quick-growing tree aloe that forms a ten-foot trunk crowned with a rosette of long, narrow, sharply pointed leaves. The flower spikes are tall, simple, and covered with myriad yellow and orange bells in early spring. The finest of the tree aloes, however, is *A. ferox,* a magnificent plant whose thick trunk rises fifteen feet to a broad rosette of exceptionally spiny, dull green leaves. The flower spikes have as many as ten candelabra-like arms carrying thousands of glowing scarlet blossoms. It is no wonder that this stately plant has been made the national floral emblem of South Africa.

All the aloes are strong plants, with no special cultural problems, pests, or diseases. They will grow in almost any soil, provided it is well drained. For the most part they appreciate an open, sunny location indoors or out. The only exceptions are those species with very dark green or heavily spotted foliage, such as *A. variegata.* These plants do best when given morning sun and afternoon shade, or partial shade all day.

While some species, such as *A. africana,* can take temperatures to 20°F., most aloes are relatively tender plants and must be protected from freezing. Contrary to the usual rule, young plants and the newer portions of old plants seem less severely damaged by frosts than the older, more solid parts. Actually it is best to discard most aloes after twenty or twenty-five years because young plants have better form and produce more and larger flower spikes.

Aloes are easily propagated by seed, divisions, or cuttings. Unfortunately they cross so readily that unless pollination is controlled propagation by seed is unlikely to give the particular species desired. The seeds germinate readily, however, and some species make good blooming plants in three years.

Since many aloes form clumps containing numerous plants, these may be readily divided and planted separately. But with species that do not cluster freely, such as the large shrubby and treelike forms, the head of the plant may be cut off with a short piece of the trunk, dried for a week or two, and rooted again in the ground. Heads weighing up to fifty pounds have been rerooted in this way and usually bloom again the first year. And, finally, some species occasionally produce small plants on their flower stalks. These may be cut off, with a bit of the stalk attached, and rooted like cuttings.

The Genus Gasteria. It is not surprising that members of

OTHER SUCCULENT FAMILIES

THE LILY FAMILY

the South African genus *Gasteria* (gas-tee'-ri-ah) are among the handsomest of all succulents, for they are very closely related to the aloes. All the fifty or more species have stiff, tongue-shaped leaves, often wonderfully smooth and marbled with white or jeweled with tiny wartlike tubercles. From these they get their popular name, Ox Tongue.

Unlike the aloes, the gasterias do not always form symmetrical rosettes. Sometimes their flat leaves are arranged in two opposite rows with the ends tipped up to make a plant that looks like an open letter U; sometimes the U is twisted to form a spiral; but when the leaves are heavy and triangular they are usually grouped in a true rosette.

The flowers also differ from those of the aloes. They hang loosely on tall, gracefully curving spikes; the colors are soft pinks and reds tipped with green; and there is a characteristic bulge at the base of each tubular bloom. On the whole, gasterias are much smaller plants too, wonderfully suited to pot culture in the home. Their strange forms, handsome foliage, and easy bloom have made them prime favorites with gardeners everywhere.

It is sometimes difficult to recommend particular gasteria species, however, for they have crossed so freely among themselves and the aloes that the list of varieties and forms seems almost endless. But it is worth while to remember that virtually any and all plants in this genus are good and worth growing.

Of the species with two-ranked leaves *G. verrucosa* is probably the best known. It is especially admired for its tapering six-inch leaves, which take on shades of pink and purple in winter and are covered the year round with innumerable pearly-white tubercles. But the handsomest species in this group, and perhaps the whole genus, is *G. maculata.* Its smooth, glossy, dark green leaves are beautifully spotted with white and gracefully twisted in a loose spiral. Although it is not a large plant, its branched flower stalk is nearly four feet high and bears countless scarlet bells.

G. carinata is a good example of those gasterias that have somewhat triangular, fleshy leaves arranged in true rosette form. Its leaves are about six inches long, a dull green studded with white tubercles. One of the largest gasterias also belongs to this group, *G. acinacifolia*. It makes a very impressive rosette of fifteen-inch leaves that are a glossy, deep green irregularly spotted and marked with white.

The gasterias are unbelievably tough plants, able to withstand cramped quarters, poor light, extreme drought, and flagrant neglect. Perhaps that is why they are such popular house plants. But they do respond to good care—which means rich, well-drained soil, a little shading in summer, careful watering in winter, and protection from frost. Gasterias are easily propagated by offsets which form freely around the plants; leaf cuttings, of which even a small section will make a plant; or seeds, which unfortunately seldom come true to type.

The Genus Haworthia. The haworthias (hau-wur'-thi-ah) so nearly resemble miniature aloes that for a long time they were included in that genus. With nearly a hundred species, all native to South Africa, the haworthias present a delightful variety of plant forms.

Some species form low rosettes of firm, dark leaves edged with teeth and covered with warty tubercles. Others develop an erect, columnar plant that is entirely covered with short, pointed, overlapping leaves arranged in spiral rows from the ground up. Still others form low rosettes of soft leaves that are "windowed" with translucent streaks towards the tips. These windows permit sunlight to enter the body of the plant even though it may be almost entirely buried underground in periods of intense heat and drought. Indeed, it is for these fascinating plant forms that the haworthias have become prized house plants, for their tiny greenish-white flowers are, frankly speaking, inconspicuous.

All species of haworthias make the neatest, most interesting pot plants imaginable, indoors or out. Among plants of the first type described one might select at random the charming Zebra Haworthia, *H. fasciata,* whose dainty dark green leaves are distinctively banded crosswise with neat rows of white tubercles. Or we might choose the equally popular and beautiful *H. margaritifera,* whose six-inch rosettes of sharply pointed leaves are sprinkled with myriad pearly-white granules.

Of the taller-growing, columnar species no collection can afford to miss *H. reinwardtii,* a magnificent plant whose numerous closely packed leaves seem encrusted with white pearls. And for contrast we can take the plain, dark green leaves of *H. viscosa,* which form a stiff triangular column nearly six inches high.

And, finally, nothing can match the windowed haworthias for sheer interest. Here we might choose the plump *H. retusa,* whose fleshy, pale green leaves are so curiously flattened and translucent at their tips, or the very prolific *H. cymbiformis.* But the most amazing species of all is *H. truncata,* whose leaves are two-ranked like a gasteria and abruptly cut off at the windowed tips as if by a knife.

All that was said for the culture of gasterias applies to the haworthias as well. They need protection from frost, good drainage, and careful watering in winter. The hard-leaved species will stand more sun than the soft-leaved kinds, but all are better with a little shade in summer. Propagation is easy from offsets which are freely produced by most species; by leaf cuttings, which are rather more difficult; and by seed, which is of doubtful value as the plants hybridize so readily.

The Minor Genera. There are several lesser genera of succulent plants in the Lily family which are occasionally seen in amateur collections. The genus *Apicra* (ah-py'-krah), for example, is so closely related to the columnar haworthias that it is very difficult to tell them apart when they are not in flower. Apicra blooms are regular, however, while haworthia flowers are irregular: that is, their three upper petals are larger than their three lower ones. Of a dozen or more species native to Cape Province only one is commonly grown, *A. pentagona,* a trim little plant with sharp, pale green leaves forming a spiral column almost a foot high.

Another South African genus consisting of a handful of more or less succulent plants is *Bulbine* (bul-by'-nee). *B. alooides* is a very soft, aloelike plant with smooth, pale green leaves forming rosettes a foot in diameter. Its feathery yellow flowers are produced on long stems in spring. *B. caulescens* forms a two-foot shrub with very narrow, pale green leaves. The culture given gasterias and haworthias is adequate for both *Bulbine* and *Apicra.*

The greatest novelty among all succulents, however, belongs to the tiny South African genus *Bowiea* (boh'-ee-ah). Its single species, *B. volubilis,* is a large, pale green, succulent bulb up to eight inches in diameter which grows half buried in the soil. From it each year come one or more long, thin, twining stems that are profusely branched and in some ways resemble a bright green ornamental asparagus. The few scale-like leaves that form above the bulb soon drop, and these stems take over the functions of leaves. On them too are borne myriad tiny greenish-white flowers and seeds.

Bowiea volubilis is truly a remarkable plant. Its huge onionlike bulbs have been known to make their annual growth for four consecutive years while stored on a bare museum shelf. Certainly no one could ask for a tougher, stranger succulent than this. A well-grown plant, attractively trained on a trellis, cannot fail to become the center of attraction in any collection.

Bowiea usually begins its strange growth in fall. The bulbs should be potted in a rich, light soil and kept warm and well watered until the stems mature in late spring. Then water is gradually withheld and the plants kept quite dry through the summer months. Propagation is by seeds, which are formed quite freely, or by natural division of the bulbs.

The Mesembryanthemum Family—The *Aizoaceae*

Fifty years ago the mesembryanthemums (mes-em-bri-an'-the-mum) were considered simply a large genus in the *Aizoaceae* (ay-eye-zoh-ay'-see-ee), or Carpetweed, family, the only other member of any importance being the genus *Tetragonia,* which provides our summer gardens with New Zealand Spinach. But after the turn of the century new explorations in South Africa disclosed that the mesembryanthemums were not only the most important genus in the Carpetweed family but one of the largest groups of succulents in the world. Almost overnight the genus *Mesembryanthemum* grew from three hundred species to more than two thousand. And, as had happened with the Cactus, it became obvious that some better method of classification must be found for the myriad plant forms and varieties the bulging genus now contained. In time it was divided into more than one hundred and fifty new genera, each according to its special characteristics of flower and fruit, and the old generic name *Mesembryanthemum* was retained for only a small group of shrubby species. Now it has been suggested that these one hundred and fifty new genera be removed from the Carpetweed family entirely and put in a new family called the *Mesembryanthemaceae.*

Despite these scientific changes, however, popular usage still clings to the old name *mesembryanthemum,* sometimes shortened to "mesemb," to refer to many plants in this family which have long since been renamed. Of course it is well-nigh impossible for the amateur to remember all the new names and fine distinctions that separate one genus from another, but he can learn to identify the four main classes of plants in this family at once. First, there are the erect, much-branched shrubby species, with succulent leaves and woody stems that grow up to two or three feet high. Second, the creeping, mat-forming types that rarely grow over a foot high but have very long semi-woody stems and fleshy leaves. Third, the compact, nearly stemless species whose succulent leaves are grouped close together to form short tufts or clusters only a few inches high. And fourth, the very small, highly succulent forms which often consist of only a single pair of leaves and are stone mimics or "windowed" plants.

In addition to these varied plant forms the mesembryanthemums possess some of the most beautiful and brilliant flowers among all succulents. At first glance they resemble daisies, but closer examination shows them to be a single flower, not a head composed of a cluster of flowers, as in the *Compositae*. Despite their botanical name, which originally meant "noon-flowers," mesembryanthemums do not bloom only in the sunny hours, but in late afternoon and evening as well. Their colors defy description, for they range through every brilliant tint and shade, every electric combination of white, yellow, pink, red, and purple imaginable. They are generally large and produced with such lavish abandon that their effect is truly dazzling.

The fruit of the mesembryanthemums is a five-sided capsule with an ingenious system of valves to regulate its opening. Unlike most seed pods, which open when dry, the mesembryanthemums open only when wet. Because the areas they inhabit often receive no rain for two or three years, this water-operated release insures there will be enough moisture for germination when the seeds fall to earth. The capsules can be made to open at will, however, by soaking them in water for a few minutes, at which time the valves will lift and expose the small seeds below.

The brief summary which follows cannot describe all the

miraculous devices and forms the collector will find in this amazing group of South African leaf succulents. But it can outline the four major groups again with some of the outstanding genera and species included in them.

The Shrubby Mesembryanthemums. There are probably no more familiar or popular succulents in all the world than the shrubby mesembryanthemums. In almost every desert playground, every warm seaside resort these plants display their flowers in dazzling sheets of color the year round. And in colder climates too they are among the most spectacular plants for rockeries and borders, pots and window boxes all summer long. Indeed, they have been so widely grown and loved that amateurs and nurserymen alike still call them by their old generic name, *Mesembryanthemum,* though they have long been separated into several distinct genera.

Perhaps the most beautiful of these shrubby "mesembryanthemums" are found in the genus *Lampranthus* (lam-pran'-thus), which forms bushy plants a foot or two high with narrow, fleshy leaves and exceptionally showy flowers about two inches in diameter. Some of its outstanding species are *L. coccineus,* with glowing scarlet flowers; *L. aureus,* a splendid pot plant with bright orange flowers; *L. conspicuus, spectabilis,* and *zeyheri* with rich red-purple blooms; *L. roseus,* a lovely, soft rose pink; and *L. brownii,* whose flowers open burnt orange, then slowly change to bright purple.

In marked contrast the genus *Oscularia* (os-keu-lay'-ri-ah) is grown more for the striking shape and color of its leaves than its flowers. It makes a rather low, shrubby growth, about a foot high, with attractive red stems and chubby, triangular, gray-green leaves. In the species *O. caulescens* the plant is slightly taller and looser, with smooth leaves; in *O. deltoides* it is more compact, with toothed leaves; and in *O. deltoides* var. *muricata,* it is very dwarf and dense, with shorter, smaller leaves that are heavily toothed. All these species produce numerous half-inch pink flowers in spring.

Another popular genus of dwarf, bushy "mesembs" is *Delosperma* (del-oh-spur'-ma). Certainly the best known of its one hundred small, densely clustered, free-flowering species is *D. echinatum.* This is a very distinct little shrub, about a foot high, whose green, fleshy, oval leaves are covered with beautiful glistening white tubercles and hairs, above which are displayed creamy-white, half-inch flowers the year round.

But the most remarkably jeweled leaves belong to the genus *Drosanthemum* (dro-san'-the-mum), for here the glistening tubercles are so numerous and bright that the plants seem bathed in dew. *D. floribundum* is an old favorite that has long been used as a low ground cover on dry banks and slopes in mild climates. Its thin, trailing branches are closely strung with tiny, pale green, cylindrical leaves and display a solid mass of half-inch pale pink flowers in summer. But the finest of all is *D. speciosum,* which forms an erect, bright green shrub nearly two feet high, smothered with two-inch red-orange flowers that have a brilliant green eye. It is probably the most spectacular of all shrubby mesembryanthemums and a "must" for every collection.

The Trailing Mesembryanthemums. It is very difficult to draw a strict line of demarcation between the shrubby and trailing mesembryanthemums, for as we have seen in *Drosanthemum floribundum,* a genus may contain plants of both habits. But on the whole, there are certain genera which are quite distinctly prostrate and are used primarily as ground cover and trailing plants.

Perhaps the most familiar trailing mesembryanthemum is that old garden annual the Ice Plant, *Cryophytum crystallinum* (kry-oh-fy'-tum), whose flat, fleshy leaves and creeping stems are covered with transparent tubercles that look like ice crystals, but are in reality water reservoirs and heat reflectors. It has naturalized itself in sandy places along the coasts of California and Lower California, Africa and the Mediterranean, and become so commonplace that the name Ice Plant has sometimes been carelessly applied to all trailing mesembryanthemums. Certainly its one-inch white flowers are not especially striking, but its glistening foliage makes an attractive drapery for a sunny wall or bank, a hanging basket or window box anywhere.

Another familiar group of prostrate mesembryanthemums is found in the genus *Carpobrotus* (kahr-po-broh'-tus), which have also become naturalized near the sea in all the warmer regions of the world. The carpobroti are large, trailing perennials with very long stems set with fleshy, triangular, bright green leaves that are often tinged with red. Their flowers are the largest in the family, averaging four or five inches in diameter, and some species bear large edible fruit. Perhaps the commonest of these is *C. edulis,* the Hottentot Fig, whose four-inch flowers range from yellow to pink. Somewhat similar is the Sea Fig, *C. chilensis,* whose rosy-purple flowers make a vivid splash of color from our Pacific Coast to Chile. And, finally, *C. acinaciformis,* whose five-inch carmine flowers are the largest in the entire Mesembryanthemum family. All these species are very quick-growing, rather coarse, and sometimes untidy; but they are unexcelled for holding drifting sand, newly cut banks, or dirt fills in hot, dry, marginal areas that are seldom watered.

Members of the genus *Hymenocyclus* (hi'-men-oh-sik'-lus) are equally valuable as coarse, rank-growing ground covers, but they provide in addition much more attractive foliage the year round. The narrow, light green leaves form great spreading masses about a foot high covered with rather modest yellow, orange, or bronze flowers. Worthwhile species are *H. croceus,* yellow; *H. herrei,* yellow orange; and *H. purpureo-croceus,* reddish purple centered yellow.

Though they can cover considerable areas when grown in the open, plants in the genus *Cephalophyllum* (sef'-ah-lohfil'-um) are of far more refined habit than any of these. Their long, cylindrical or triangular leaves are clustered in rosettes along prostrate stems; and their handsome flowers, produced from midwinter through summer, are truly exceptional. Many consider the vibrant red-purple blooms of *C. alstonii* the most beautiful flowers in the entire Mesembryanthemum family. And equally fine, though produced on a much larger plant, are the lovely, four-inch, salmon-pink blooms of *C. spongiosum*. But the prize for originality must go to *C. tricolorum*, whose two-inch yellow flowers are stained purple at the base, red at the tip, and display a cluster of red filaments topped with brown anthers.

Most of these shrubby and trailing mesembryanthemums are standard landscape plants in the arid western and southwestern United States, but they have not yet been used as much as they deserve in the East. They are eminently suitable for summer bedding in hot, dry areas of the flower garden, for pots and window boxes, or for seaside plantings. Although they must usually be started again each year from seeds or cuttings in colder climates, they grow so quickly and bloom so profusely that they are well-nigh indispensable for the busy summer gardener who would have a brilliant flower display with little water or work.

The Clustering Mesembryanthemums. While the shrubby and trailing mesembryanthemums are extremely valuable to the landscaper and home gardener, the clustering mesembryanthemums are of greater importance to the collector of succulents. Their odd forms and neat habit make them ideal plants for succulent collections indoors or out, and their easy culture and handsome bloom are extra dividends no beginner can afford to overlook.

The transition from the trailing mesembryanthemums to the clustering types is perhaps most clearly seen in the genus *Glottiphyllum* (glot-i-fil'-um). The glottiphyllums are dwarf succulent plants somewhat reminiscent of the coarse trailing mesembryanthemums, but they have virtually no stems at all, only cylindrical or tongue-shaped leaves united in pairs, each two or three pairs forming a short growth. In the very popular species *G. linguiforme,* the Tongue Leaf, the leaves are very fleshy, tongue-shaped, a bright glossy green, and form a crowded clustering plant topped with bright yellow three-inch flowers.

Another low, clustering genus especially admired for its oddly shaped and roughened leaves is *Hereroa* (her-er-oh'-ah). The upright plants quickly form clumps of soft, triangular, incurved leaves that are often pebbled with tiny raised dots and sometimes curiously flattened and notched at the tips. This latter characteristic is so prominent in the popular *H. dyeri* that it has earned the descriptive title Elk's Horns. In the same way the curving, sickle-shaped leaves of *H. nelii* so nearly resemble a Shriner's badge that it has been called the Shriner's Plant. All the hereroas are extremely easy and interesting plants for the beginner and offer a wealth of yellow flowers in spring and summer.

Although the genus *Trichodiadema* (tri-kod'-i-ah-dee'-mah) contains plants of shrubby and trailing habit too, it is best known for its clustering species. These are very low-stemmed, compact little plants with tiny cylindrical leaves that are tipped with a crown of cactus-like bristles. Perhaps the best-known species is the Desert Rose, *T. densum,* whose tufted three-inch plants spring from a carrot-like root and are topped with exceptionally handsome, two-inch, violet-pink flowers.

But of all the clustering mesembryanthemums none has been so widely grown and loved as the delightful species of *Faucaria* (faw-kay'-ree-ah). The faucarias form low rosettes consisting of pairs of fleshy, triangular leaves that resemble the gaping jaws of an animal, because they usually display prominent white teeth along their inner margins. This accounts for the common name Tiger Jaws which is given the most popular species, *F. tigrina,* a very elegant little gray-green plant that is heavily spotted with white and bears fine

OTHER SUCCULENT FAMILIES

THE MESEMBRYANTHEMUM FAMILY

two-inch yellow flowers. Other good species are the Knobby Tiger Jaws, *F. tuberculosa,* with very thick, warty, dark green leaves; and the Waxy Tiger Jaws, *F. bosscheana,* with small, glossy green leaves margined with white. Actually any of the forty or more species of *Faucaria* are well worth growing, not only for their neat clustering plants but for their surprisingly large yellow autumn flowers.

The last genus of clustering mesembryanthemums we must consider is *Cheiridopsis* (ky-ree-dop'-sis). Virtually all its ninety or more species are great favorites because they are interesting, compact plants well suited to pot culture. The cheiridopses make short growths consisting of one to three pairs of opposite leaves, each pair different in form, size, and growth from the others. Thus on one plant the young top leaves may be erect and close together, the pair below large and wide-spreading, and the old leaves at the bottom dried into a sort of sheath which served to protect the younger growths during the resting period. This characteristic of the old, papery-white leaves protecting the new is especially evident in *C. meyeri,* which looks like nothing more than a handful of white pebbles thrown on the ground during its resting season. In the species *C. cigarettifera* the dry sheaths of the old leaves resemble the mouthpiece of a cigarette out of which rises the slender, erect, new growth. And there are many other interesting and valuable species, such as *C. pillansii,* which really lives up to its popular name, Lobster Claws; and the amazing, rocklike *C. peculiaris,* which is very aptly named too. But the finest of them all is the Victory Plant, *C. candidissima,* whose four-inch white leaves stand erect in V-shaped pairs topped by the most beautiful soft-pink flowers imaginable.

The Stone-Mimicry and Windowed Mesembryanthemums. It is only a short way from the low, rocklike clusters of the cheiridopses to the true stone-mimicry and windowed plants of the Mesembryanthemum family, but that way leads to some of the most interesting and highly developed succulents in all the world. Because they inhabit the driest parts of South Africa, where at times rain does not fall once in two years, these plants have perfected the devices of succulence to the highest possible degree.

They have reduced themselves to one or two pairs of thick, fleshy leaves to serve as perfect water reservoirs. They have become nearly round in shape to contain the greatest volume of moisture with the least possible surface exposed to evaporation. They have learned to lie low in the long months of drought with their new growths wrapped in a papery envelope of old leaves, or buried in the soil with only the leaf tips exposed. And to compensate for burying themselves in this way—which puts their breathing pores and chlorophyll cells underground, where air and sunlight cannot reach them—they have learned to transpire through their sides and to admit sunlight to their green cells within through translucent windows developed in their leaf tips exposed aboveground. But despite these wonders the most remarkable feats of these plants lie in the realm of protective imitation, camouflage, and mimicry.

We are all familiar with protective form and coloring among animals and insects, and we have even seen instances of mimicry among the Living Rock Cacti. But the most numerous and perfect mimics in all the plant world are the stone mimics of the Mesembryanthemum family. In order to survive in their rainless habitat these plants have not only had to economize, store, and lie low, but protect themselves from the thirsty desert animals who would devour them instantly for their juicy flesh. Without the defense of spines or teeth, a tough skin or unpleasant taste, they have chosen instead to simulate the rocks and pebbles among which they grow. And so nearly do they resemble these stones in color, texture, and shape that they are practically invisible in their native habitat except when in bloom. Fortunately this brief blooming period occurs only during the rainy season, when all other vegetation is abundant and there is sufficient food for browsing animals everywhere. When the rains cease and the countryside dries again, the stone mimics quietly blend into the land once more.

Remarkable as this camouflage is, however, it must be understood that these plants have not consciously imitated their surroundings. It is actually a case of "survival of the fittest." For over millions of years those stone-mimicry plants which could not easily be seen by predators have remained, propagated themselves, and been improved by natural selection until they have achieved this almost perfect means of protection.

Of the twenty or more genera containing stone-mimicry plants, windowed plants, or both, the genus *Pleiospilos* (ply-oh-spy'-los) is easily the most popular. The pleiospiles are all stone-mimicry plants consisting of one or more pairs of very thick, distinctly separate, brownish gray-green leaves. These leaves are often angular in shape and covered with darker raised spots which give them a rough appearance, like the bits of weathered granite among which they grow. Although they may reach the size of a duck egg and often grow in large clusters, these leaves are virtually invisible as they lie half buried among the rocks until the showy two- or three-inch flowers appear. *Pleiospilos bolusii* is perhaps the best-known species in amateur collections, where its very heavy, angular, rocklike leaves make a plant four inches in diameter displaying golden yellow flowers in fall. Two other species that are very similar and equally fine are the African Living Rock, *P. simulans,* with longer, wider-opening leaves; and *P. nelii,* the Split Rock, with more compact, smoothly rounded leaves and bright, bronze-orange flowers in spring.

To many the most fascinating of all mimicry and windowed plants are the seventy-odd species of the genus *Lithops* (lith'-ops). They are all very small, cylindrical or conical plants, averaging only an inch or an inch and a half in height, and consist simply of a pair of closely united, fleshy, flat-topped leaves separated by a cleft. In nature these plants are buried among rocks and pebbles so that only their tops are visible, and on these tops, or Stone Faces, each species is distinctively windowed, marked, and colored to blend with its surroundings. Some lithops are solitary, some clustering, but all produce surprisingly large flowers an inch or more in diameter in autumn. After flowering and seeding, the plants become dormant and wither, whiten and break open, and a fresh pair of leaves emerge to form a new plant body for the coming year. It is well-nigh impossible to mention all the wonderful species and varieties available, but no collection should miss *L. aucampiae,* a rather large, brick-red species with yellow blossoms; *L. bella,* a handsome yellow-brown species with white flowers; *L. comptonii,* olive green with yellow flowers; *L. fulleri,* pearl gray and brown with white flowers; *L. lesliei,* olive brown and rust with yellow blooms; and, best of all, *L. pseudotruncatella,* a fine beige-gray and brown plant with golden-yellow flowers.

In some ways the genus *Conophytum* (ko-nof'-i-tum) resembles *Lithops,* but in many more it differs from it. All its two hundred and fifty or more species are formed of two fleshy leaves, but these leaves are completely united and only a short slit is left at the top for flowering. Its plant bodies are of three different forms: rounded, cone-shaped with a flat top, or flat-sided with a bilobed top. They range from pea size to four inches in length and form clusters of several to many heads. The conophytums, or Cone Plants, do not bury themselves, but owe their invisibility entirely to their shape and color, which resemble the grayish, veined, and marbled pebbles among which they grow. Their autumn flowers have a greater range of color—white, cream, yellow, orange, red, pink, and purple—and their petals are united at the base into a slender tube so that each flower stands like a little umbrella atop the plants. But like the lithops, the conophytums go through a very distinct growth cycle each year. The new plant body forms inside the old, draws on it for sustenance, breaks through its withered remains at the beginning of the growing season, flowers, forms seed, and completes its cycle by nurturing another young plant within itself for the coming year. Unfortunately the conophytums are not very well represented in American collections, and relatively few species are available to the beginner. Of these he might choose *C. braunsii,* with its small, flat-topped, clustering plants and bright magenta-pink flowers; *C. giftbergensis,* with pale green, grape-like clusters and yellow blooms; *C. minutum,* a very tiny gray-green species which forms thick clumps a half inch high topped with purple flowers; or *C. meyerae,* one of the rare bilobed conophytums, whose forked two-inch growths and yellow flowers are somewhat difficult but interesting.

These twin factors of difficulty and availability must necessarily limit any excursion into the stone-mimicry and windowed mesembryanthemums, for while their number is legion they are not all easy or accessible to the beginner. Of the genera that remain we might pick a few plants at random, however, that are within the reach of any collector.

Among the stone-mimicry plants there are several genera whose members grow in white quartz soil, so they have taken on a white, gray, or bluish coloring that makes them almost invisible. Perhaps the finest of these are the Silverskins, members of the genus *Argyroderma* (ar'-ji-roh-dur'-mah), whose plants consist of only two, rounded, silvery-white leaves with a deep cleft between that match perfectly the broken pieces of white quartz among which they grow. *A. octophyllum,* with yellow blossoms, is perhaps the most popular; *A. roseum,* with three-inch rose-violet flowers, the most spectacular; and *A. braunsii,* with long, finger-like leaves, the strangest. Very much like the argyrodermas, and once classed with them, is the popular Karroo Rose, *Lapidaria margaretae* (lap-i-day'-

ri-ah), a small pearl-gray plant suffused with pink and bearing two-inch yellow flowers in winter. Still pursuing this type of mimicry, species of the genus *Gibbaeum* (ji-bee'-um) owe their whiteness to a close covering of microscopic hairs that make the plants look like a pile of white quartz slivers. They are easily distinguished from other stone-mimicry plants, however, by their two closely pressed unequal leaves, which give the plants an uneven profile, like a Shark's Head, hence their popular name. *G. album* is a small species with very beautiful white leaves and white flowers; *G. heathii* has heavy, paired, greenish-white leaves like a pleiospilos; and *G. shandii,* long, narrow, gray-white leaves and bright red-purple flowers.

The last important type of stone mimicry among the mesembryanthemums is found in the genus *Titanopsis* (ty-ta-nop'-sis), a group of small, rosette-forming plants whose leaves are covered with irregular white warts that match the weathered incrustations on the limestone fragments among which they grow. *T. calcarea,* the Jewel Plant, is the best-known species, forming a compressed two-inch rosette of blue-green to purple leaves studded with gray- or rosy-white tubercles and bright golden-yellow flowers.

Of windowed plants in various genera no collector should miss the two popular species that make up the genus *Fenestraria* (fen-es-tray'-ree-ah). They are both small, light green, club-shaped, clustering plants with very prominent, glassy, "windowed" tips. The popular name Baby Toes is apt for either species: *F. aurantiaca,* with one-inch plants and three-inch orange-yellow flowers; or *F. rhopalophylla,* with shorter plants and one-inch white flowers. The single species of the genus *Frithia* (frith'-i-ah), *Frithia pulchra,* is very much like the fenestrarias but somewhat smaller, with duller windows, and more difficult to grow; but its bright magenta flowers, centered white, last for two or three weeks at a time and are well worth the extra effort. And finally, midway between

Lithops and *Conophytum,* we find the delightful genus *Ophthalmophyllum* (of-thal'-mo-fil'-um). It contains beautiful little plants generally like *Lithops* in appearance and *Conophytum* in growth habit, with very bright windowed tops. *O. friedrichiae* makes a smooth green plant about one inch high that turns copper red during the resting period; *O. maughanii,* a larger, pale green plant with yellow-green windows and white flowers; and *O. herrei,* a velvety olive-green plant with fragrant white flowers tipped with pink.

The cultural requirements of these mesembryanthemums vary as widely as their spread over South Africa. While they all require protection from frost, maximum sunlight, and free ventilation, their needs in soil, water, and drainage are still governed largely by the growing conditions of their original habitat. The shrubby and trailing mesembryanthemums are certainly not difficult to grow with almost any soil or treatment, but as one moves into the more specialized types the need for careful handling and observation becomes imperative. This does not mean that the clustering, stone-mimicry, or windowed mesembryanthemums are especially difficult, but they do require more careful treatment if they are to retain their unique forms and habits, cycles of growth and rest.

A basic soil mixture for these very succulent types consists of two parts coarse sand, one part decayed leaf mold, and one part soil, to which another part of pea gravel or stone chips should be added to give even sharper drainage and enhance the effect of these stone-mimicry and windowed plants. The latter, by the way, should not be buried deep in the soil as in their native habitat, but allowed to stand up out of the surrounding pebbles so that they are more clearly visible and less susceptible to rot.

The danger of rotting is very great in cultivation, as these plants grow actively and need water for only a few months of the year and must be kept quite dry during the resting months. Since seasons, temperatures, and cultural conditions vary widely in every locality, it is impossible to say definitely when any given plant should be watered or rested. The best guide is the condition of the plant itself. When the resting period begins, usually with the coming of hot weather in summer, the plants take on a dull, lifeless look. They may shrivel to a papery skin, like the conophytums, or withdraw deeper into the soil, like the lithops; but as soon as the papery skin cracks, showing that a new growth is on its way or the plants take on a fresher color in the cool autumn days, normal watering may be resumed once again. Of course the plants are not kept bone-dry during the resting period, but watered very sparingly to keep them alive but not active, barely moistened but not rotted.

The propagation of mesembryanthemums is generally very easy. All types may be grown from seed, sown in spring or fall, if it is available and true to name. Shrubby and trailing species may be propagated by stem cuttings the year round, but the more succulent types are best rooted about a month before the growing season starts. It is important that cuttings of the smaller species consist of a complete plant body with a bit of the stem attached, as slices of leaves will not root. Occasionally the clustering species may be divided, but it is important here too that each division have part of the original stem attached or roots of its own.

The Milkweed Family—The *Asclepiadaceae*

Few gardeners realize that the *Asclepiadaceae* (as-klee-pee-a-day'-see-ee), or Milkweed family, with two hundred and fifty genera and two thousand species, contains not only the common milky-juiced perennials we call milkweeds, but such choice ornamental plants as the Wax Vine, *Hoya carnosa;* the Madagascar Jasmine, *Stephanotis floribunda;* and a wealth of fine succulents native to semi-arid regions from India and the Middle East to Africa and Spain. These succulent milkweeds are largely found in two tribes, the *Stapelieae* (stap-eh-li′-ee-ee) and the *Ceropegieae* (see-roh-peej′-ee-ee), both of unusual interest to succulent collectors.

The Stapelia Tribe. The twenty genera and nearly four hundred species of the Stapelia (stah-pee′-li-ah) tribe are among the most curious of all succulent plants. They are all stem succulents, branching from the base to form tiny tufted plants an inch or two high up to large bushes three feet or more in height, but the greatest number rarely grow more than a foot tall. Their smooth, thick, succulent stems vary in cross section from circular to many-angled, the majority being four- or six-angled. Along these angles, or ribs, are borne innumerable fleshy teeth, or tubercles, which mark the position of the primitive leaves which have long since disappeared from every member of this tribe save one, *Frerea indica* (free′-ree-ah), a rare leafy ancestral type that is to the Stapeliads what the *Pereskia* is to the Cacti.

Even more striking than the plants, however, which actually seem very much like cacti to the beginner, are the unique flowers. The blossoms of this tribe are generally in the form of a five-pointed star, sometimes widely expanded, sometimes closed to form a saucer or bell. They range from miniatures less than an inch in diameter to giants eighteen inches across that rank among the world's largest flowers. But more important than shape or size are the strange colors and odors of these blooms. Most of them look and smell for all the world like rotting fish or meat, hence their popular name, Carrion Flowers.

The reason for this curious adaptation in color and odor is that these plants are pollinated by blowflies, which are attracted to the flowers in great numbers and lay their eggs on the petals under the impression that they are bits of putrid meat. Although the maggots may hatch they cannot survive, for there is nothing here for them to feed on. The lurid brown, red, or yellow petals which are so ingeniously marked or fringed with animal-like hairs serve only to lure the insects by sight as well as smell.

This dependence on flies for pollination is due largely to the unusual construction of the flowers in this family. The pollen grains of the Milkweeds are not loose and easily scattered by wind or chance, as they are in many other plants but, as in the orchids, are formed into waxy bodies which cannot be transferred without the aid of insects. To complicate matters further, in the Milkweeds these tiny pollen bodies are firmly attached in pairs with clamplike organs called pollen carriers. As the flies are attracted to the heart of the flowers by sight and scent and try to probe the center of the blossom, their snouts or legs become caught in the pincer-like pollen carriers. The frightened insects struggle to pull free and come away with the waxy pollen masses attached to their bodies. They carry these masses to the next flower and the next, where the process is repeated until pollination takes place.

Another interesting feature of this tribe is that the fruits do not develop until long after flowering. They usually appear the following year as twin torpedo-shaped capsules which split along one side to reveal numerous seeds each with a parachute of silky hairs which help it become wind-borne.

Certainly the best known of the Stapeliads is the genus called *Stapelia.* There are about one hundred species and varieties of this popular succulent, virtually all of them native to South Africa. The stapelias are small, clustering plants with soft, erect, four-angled stems. Most of them bear relatively large, flat, star-shaped flowers in summer which are so strangely colored and marked that they very nearly resemble starfish, hence their popular name, Starfish Flower. Almost every succulent collection begins with the common *S. variegata,* whose two-inch yellow flowers heavily spotted maroon and stubby, finger-like stems have won for it the nickname

Toad Cactus. This species has innumerable varieties, forms, and hybrids, ranging from *S. variegata* var. *cristata,* with freakish crested stems, to the handsome Black Starfish, *S. berlinensis.* Equally popular are the Hairy Starfish Flower, *S. hirsuta;* the nearly scentless Bearded Starfish Flower, *S. pulvinata,* whose four-inch blooms are wonderfully fringed with reddish-brown hairs; and *S. gettleffii,* whose exquisite six-inch flowers are creamy yellow banded with purple stripes. But the most spectacular of all are the giants of this clan—*S. nobilis,* with pale yellow-red flowers a foot across; and the Giant Starfish, *S. gigantea,* whose astounding blooms reach eighteen inches in diameter.

Very closely related to these stapelias is the genus *Caralluma* (kar-a-lu'-ma). Indeed, it is the basic genus of the tribe from which all other genera are derived. All its one hundred or more species resemble the stapelias, but with smaller flowers borne in greater profusion. The carallumas have a very wide range of distribution, from Abyssinia and Arabia to North and South Africa, and even the southwestern shores of Spain, but while they are intensely interesting plants relatively few are seen in collections. *C. europaea* and *C. burchardii* are admired for their quaintly irregular square stems and clusters of half-inch flowers, which in the latter species are covered with snowy-white hairs. This covering of sensitive, vibrating hairs is especially developed in *C. lutea,* whose three-inch canary-yellow flowers attract insects not only by color and smell, but by a continuously trembling fringe of inviting red hairs.

The fifty species of the genus *Huernia* (hur'-ni-ah), which range from southern Arabia to South Africa, are all small, neat plants with four- or five-angled stems not unlike the stapelias. But they add to the typical five-pointed star flower of the Stapeliads five smaller intermediate points, which gives them a unique, ten-pointed, bell-like flower. Outstanding species are *H. primulina,* with creamy one-inch flowers;

OTHER SUCCULENT FAMILIES

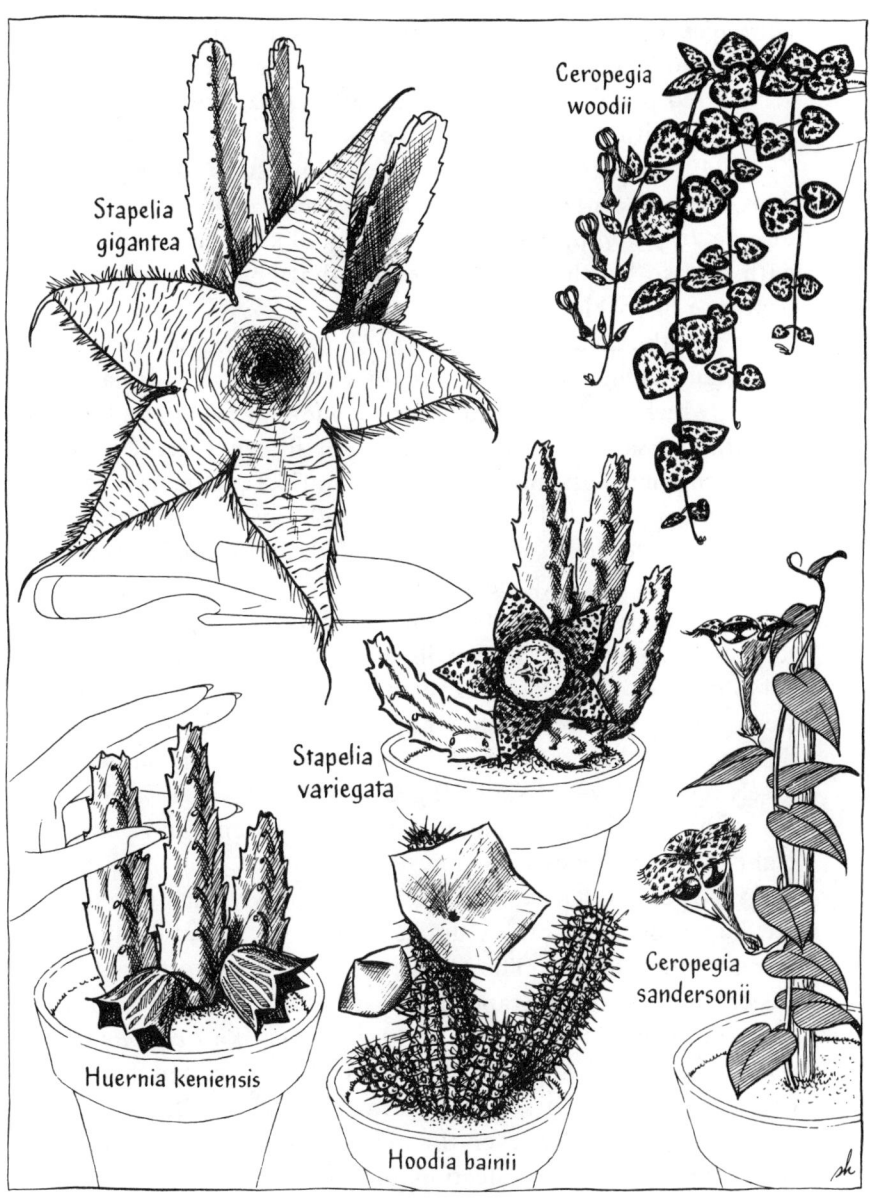

THE MILKWEED FAMILY

H. keniensis, with obtusely angled stems and little reddish-purple bells; *H. schneideriana,* the Red Dragon Flower, with velvety red petals and black center; *H. hystrix,* the Porcupine Huernia, with banded, quill-like hairs on its petals; the Zebra Flower, *H. zebrina,* whose yellow stars are striped maroon and centered with a glossy red corona; and the unique *H. pillansii,* whose twenty-angled stems are covered with myriad bristle-tipped tubercles that give them the appearance of cockleburs.

The South African genus *Hoodia* (hood'-i-ah) deserves special mention in any discussion of Stapeliads for its large plants, which often grow three feet or more in height, and for its strange, saucer-shaped flowers. All fifteen species have nearly circular blossoms in which the starlike points have virtually disappeared, leaving only small tips on the saucer edges. Despite their stout, many-angled, and toothed stems, which are, by the way, curiously reminiscent of some of the columnar cacti or euphorbias, the hoodias are rather difficult to grow and are rarely seen in collections. *H. gordoni* is a very desirable, free-blooming plant, however, with erect, spiny stems about eighteen inches high and interesting four-inch flesh-colored flowers. *H. bainii* is somewhat similar, but with lovely light yellow blossoms tinged with pink, and *H. macrantha* is the giant of the clan, with three-foot stems and bright eight-inch purple flowers.

Of the genera that remain much could be written, but some are hopelessly rare, others difficult to grow, and still others frankly uninteresting. The novice would do well to grow the easier, more popular Stapeliads first before he ventures into the more difficult kinds. To be sure, some, like *Echidnopsis cereiformis* (ek-id-nop'-sis), which is closely related to the carallumas, are relatively easy and worth while. But others have defied the skill of even the most serious collectors, and a really representative collection of Stapeliads is something more often wished than realized.

The chief difficulty in growing Stapeliads lies in judging their moisture requirements. These are rather soft, juicy plants that require light shading and moderate watering in summer and only enough moisture in winter to keep them from shriveling. Ample light and air, good drainage, and protection from frost are a "must" in all seasons. Plants that have been overfed and overwatered may sometimes develop long, snaky branches that look lush, but they are actually most susceptible to cold and rot.

Most members of the Stapelia tribe are easily raised from seed, which not only retains its vitality for many years but often germinates in only a day or two. But many species interbreed so readily that propagation by cuttings is preferred. Stem cuttings are generally taken from old plants in spring, dried thoroughly, and then rooted as other succulents. Species that are difficult to grow from cuttings or are uncommonly slow may be grafted. Either a side or flat graft is made, using *Stapelia gigantea* as an understock for thick scions and *Stapelia variegata* for slender ones. These quick-growing understocks, as well as other strong species, are themselves often propagated by simply dividing an old clump.

The Ceropegia Tribe. Although there are a number of interesting genera in this tribe, only one is commonly found in cultivation—the genus *Ceropegia* (see-roh-pee'-ji-ah). The ceropegias are very closely related to the Stapelia tribe, but come from zones of slightly higher rainfall in tropical Africa, the East Indies, and the Canary Islands. They range in form from small shrubs with succulent, leafless stems to clambering vines with tuberous roots and fleshy opposite leaves. Like the Stapeliads, their flowers are basically five-pointed stars, but with a long funnel-shaped base, above which the petals may be either separate, joined together at the tips to form a little lantern, or joined and greatly expanded to form an umbrella-like canopy.

Because the ceropegias have the characteristic waxy pollen

of the Milkweeds but not the alluring sights and smells of the Stapeliads, they have devised a clever flytrap mechanism to insure pollination. The flower tubes are usually expanded at the base and fringed inside with hairs that point downwards. Insects that venture into this pitfall cannot escape until just the moment when the pollen is ripe. Then the menacing hairs wither and the captive is free to carry off the pollen to another flower. The fruit that results is a twin pod filled with small plumed seeds, just as in the Stapeliads.

Of the shrubby ceropegias two species from the Canary Islands are occasionally seen in collections. Both have round, jointed, finger-thick stems up to three feet high which bear narrow temporary leaves during the growing season and clusters of small lantern-flowers with the petal tips united. *C. dichotoma* has three-quarter-inch pale yellow flowers, and *C. fusca* larger chocolate-brown blossoms.

Much more commonly grown are the climbing species from South Africa, such as *C. stapeliiformis.* The stout, clambering, five-foot stems of this species not only resemble a rampant stapelia, but the two-inch white flowers have separate petal tips forming a five-pointed star. Even more spectacular is the handsome *C. sandersonii,* whose strong twining stems are furnished with thick, leathery leaves and the finest flowers of the clan. These amazing blossoms are nearly three inches in length and consist of a graceful, greenish-white funnel flaring upward whose tips expand overhead to form an immense parachute-like canopy edged with vibratile hairs. It is a "must" for every serious collector.

It is scarcely necessary to recommend the several trailing species of ceropegia, for they have been favorite hanging-basket and house plants for generations. Certainly the best known is the charming, tuberous-rooted *C. woodii*—the Rosary Vine—whose slender, threadlike stems are hung with silver and green heart-shaped leaves and dainty purple lantern-flowers. Other popular trailing species somewhat like it are *C. barklyi,* with cormlike roots; *C. debilis,* with narrow, lance-shaped leaves; and *C. radicans,* with very long, slender, green-tipped flowers banded with purple and white.

The ceropegias generally require the same culture as the Stapeliads—moderate shade, warmth, and moisture in summer and a cool, dry rest in winter. Climbing species should be trained to a stake or trellis as they grow in summer lest they overtake other plants for support. All members of this tribe are easily propagated by seed, when it is available; by cuttings, which root easily at any season; or tubers, which are freely formed in the soil and along the stems of several species like *C. woodii.*

Succulents in Other Families

Besides the eight plant families outlined, which are wholly or partly succulent, there are a score or more that contain only a few succulent members. Most of these lesser succulents are rare and little-known plants, but there are a few among them that should be included in all amateur collections.

The Geranium Family—The Geraniaceae. Anyone who has observed the fleshy stems and wonderful resistance to drought of the common garden geranium will not be surprised to find that these plants have several succulent relatives in that vast South African genus *Pelargonium* (pel-ahr-goh'-ni-um), to which they also belong. These genuinely succulent geraniums are quite different from their garden cousins, however. Their stems are often greatly thickened and studded with spines. Their leaves are smaller, stand upright on long stalks, and are generally shed during the summer resting season. And their wide-open, two-lipped flowers are exquisite miniatures produced in sparse bunches.

The best-known species is *P. echinatum,* whose finger-thick, fleshy stems are covered with spinelike projections which are actually the stipules, or leaflike appendages, at the base of the fallen leaves. Only a few of these long-stalked, deciduous leaves are produced each spring with clusters of white flowers that bear two red hearts at the base of the upper petals, hence its popular name—Sweetheart Geranium. The remainder of the year this foot-high shrub looks exactly like a little cylindrical cactus.

Equally popular and interesting is *P. tetragonum.* Its spineless four-angled stems make a sprawling three-foot shrub with deciduous leaves and much larger pink flowers whose two upper petals are conspicuously veined red. Both these species need protection from frost, as well as good drainage and a dry rest in summer when the leaves have fallen. They are easily propagated by seed or cuttings in early spring or summer.

The Grape Family—The Vitaceae. Unlike the Geranium family, lush vines and grapes would not ordinarily be expected to have succulents among them, and yet there are five succulent species in the genus *Cissus* (sis'-us) of the Grape family. Three of these are true desert dwellers from Southwest Africa. Two of them thick, barrel-shaped plants two to six feet high with a topknot of deciduous leaves, the other a fleshy tree thirteen feet tall. But these are extremely rare and seldom seen in cultivation.

Much better known are two clambering shrubby species from tropical Africa, *C. quadrangularis* and *C. cactiformis.* These are both quick-growing climbers with green, four-angled, jointed stems covered with a bluish bloom. They produce a few small grapelike leaves at the joints which disappear during the summer resting period. These plants are certainly more curious than decorative, but they are collectors' items which will lend interest to any collection. They are readily propagated by cuttings and should be given the same culture as some of the Climbing Cacti, epiphyllums, and other jungle-dwelling succulents.

The Portulaca Family—The Portulacaceae. Although all the members of this family, comprising some seventeen genera

OTHER SUCCULENT FAMILIES

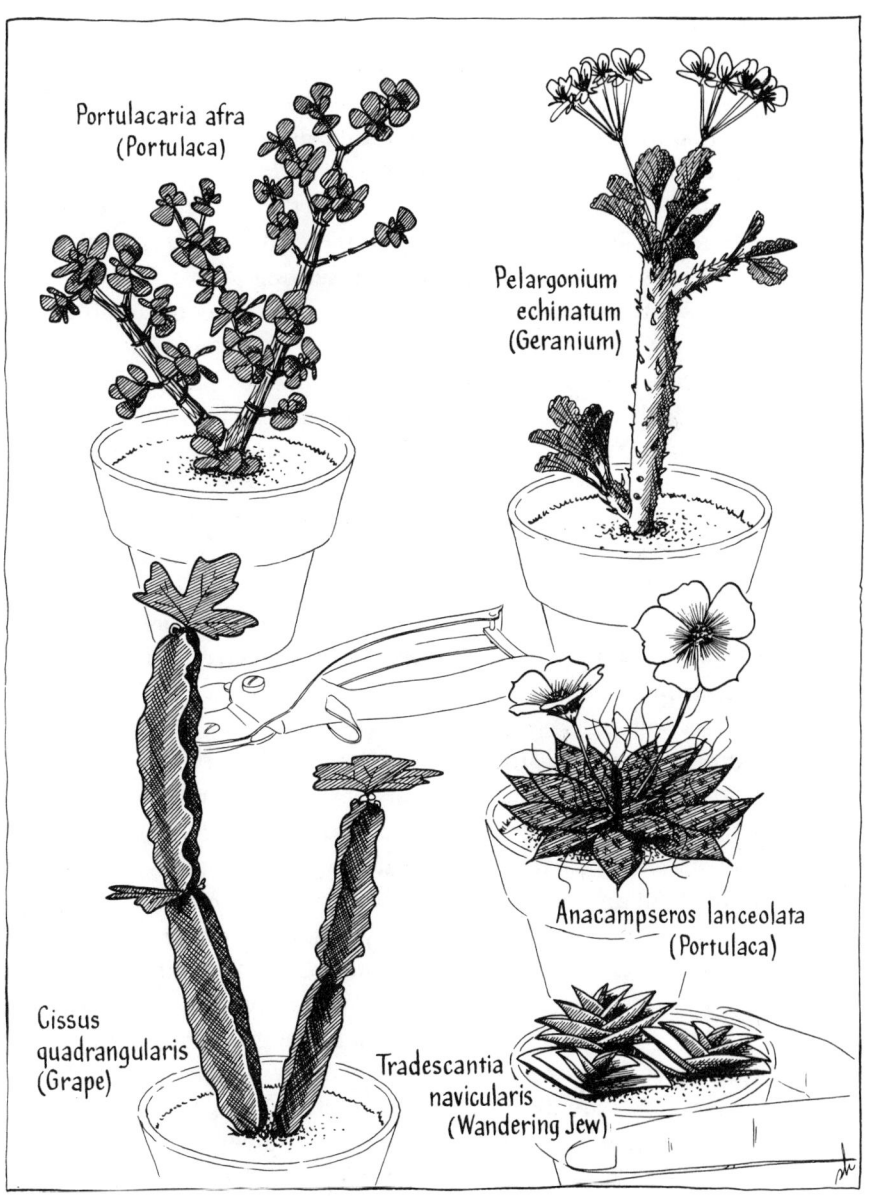

OTHER SUCCULENT FAMILIES

and two hundred species, are more or less succulent, only a few are recognized or grown as such. Everyone is familiar with the genus *Portulaca* (por-teu-lah'-kah), which gives us that wonderful trailing annual so long used for dry borders and rockeries—the Rose Moss, *P. grandiflora,* or that common summer weed Purslane, *P. oleracea,* that some curse and others relish as boiled "greens." But we do not ordinarily think of these plants as succulents, reserving that title solely for two South African genera that have gained considerable popularity with succulent collectors.

The first of these is the genus *Anacampseros* (an-a-kamp'-ser-os), which consists of two extremely interesting groups of small plants. The first group forms miniature rosettes of fat, lance-shaped, green leaves with numerous bristly hairs in the leaf axils, above which are borne little five-petaled flowers that look like single roses. Popular species of this type include the Love Plant, *A. lanceolata,* with clear pink flowers in late summer; *A. tomentosa,* with felted white leaves and red flowers; and *A. telephiastrum,* with brownish-red leaves and deep pink flowers.

The second group of anacampseros consists of plants with numerous short stems often rising from tuberous roots which bear tiny green leaves completely covered by overlapping, translucent, papery scales. These scales act somewhat like window shades, sheltering the minute, fleshy leaves within from the heat and sunlight. Because of their color and curious clustered form these plants closely resemble heaps of bird droppings, and it has been suggested that this might be a form of protective mimicry. Unfortunately this group of anacampseros is quite rare and difficult to grow, but the adventurous collector might try *A. papyracea,* whose sprawling white branches are about one half inch wide and two inches long; or *A. alstonii,* whose showy white flowers are an inch and a half across, in marked contrast to the tiny, half-concealed yellow flowers of the other species.

OTHER SUCCULENT FAMILIES

Although the first group of anacampseros is easily grown, with moderate watering and light shading in summer and a cool, dry rest in winter; the second group is extremely slow-growing and requires a very sunny position and complete drought in winter. Strangely enough, the flowers in this clan are rather shy in opening—some open for only an hour, others not at all—so that in many species the flowers are self-pollinated in the bud. Seed is freely produced, however, and is generally the best method of propagation even if slow, because cuttings can rarely be taken without spoiling the plants.

The other genus in this family which enjoys wide popularity is called *Portulacaria* (por-teu-lah-kay'-ree-ah). Its single species, *P. afra,* forms a large bush or small tree reminiscent of the shrubby crassulas, with small, glossy green leaves attached to fat, mahogany-red stems. It is a favorite food of elephants in South Africa, hence its popular name, Elephant Bush. A striking variegated form, *P. afra* var. *tricolor,* with yellow, cream, pink, and green leaves, is appropriately called the Rainbow Bush. Both these plants are easy and valuable additions to any collection, responding to good soil and ample watering by making a large, wide-spreading specimen in sun or partial shade. Since they rarely show their tiny pink flowers or make seed in cultivation, propagation is entirely by stem cuttings.

The Wandering Jew Family—The Commelinaceae. The Peruvian species, *Tradescantia navicularis* (trad-es-kan'-ti-ah), is a fascinating succulent relative of the common Wandering Jew, *T. fluminensis.* Indeed, it somewhat resembles that familiar house plant, but its tough, boat-shaped, gray-green leaves are so closely set along the stems that they have suggested the nickname Chain Plant. The prostrate stems root easily wherever they touch the ground and are topped with showy, three-lipped, rosy-purple flowers.

Very closely related to this species is an African member of the family, *Cyanotis somaliensis* (sy-ah-noh'-tis), which is often seen in succulent collections. Here we have virtually the same plant, but with larger, looser, pinkish-green leaves, which are so wonderfully hairy that they have been dubbed Pussy Ears. It produces rather small, feathery, blue flowers. Both of these interesting plants are easily propagated by cuttings or divisions and require no special care except protection from frost.

Other Families. There are many more succulent species in such families as the Pepper *(Piperaceae),* Oxalis *(Oxalidaceae),* Mulberry *(Moraceae),* Caltrop *(Zygophyllaceae),* Periwinkle *(Apocynaceae),* Passion-flower *(Passifloraceae),* Sesame *(Pedaliaceae),* and Gourd *(Cucurbitaceae),* but these are rare plants, which the amateur will see only in the finest botanical collections or as illustrations in learned books. They need not detain us here, for the story of succulents can never actually be finished.

Somewhere today imperceptible changes in temperature and rainfall, a gradual trembling and shifting of the earth, the rise of new mountains and deserts may be moving other familiar plants toward succulence. But we cannot see these changes, for the quiet miracles happening all about us may require a million years or more before we can even guess their intention. It is this sense of past, present, and future mixed that makes succulents so intensely exciting and interesting to grow. And having surveyed the wealth at our disposal, we have now only to learn how best to use and enjoy these wonderful plants in our own homes and gardens.

CHAPTER FIVE

Succulents in the Home

The current interest in house plants has led many gardeners to attempt growing all sorts of lush tropical foliage plants, ferns, and even orchids indoors. But despite their best efforts with fluorescent lights, atomizers, and humidifiers they have never been able to turn their hot, dry rooms into jungles or give the time and care these plants require. And all the while they have overlooked a whole world of plants whose magnificent forms and foliage outdo any tropical or fern, whose flowers no orchid can match, whose native habitat exceeds our rooms in heat and drought, and whose simple care even the busiest, most neglectful gardener can manage. If ever there were plants ideally suited to our modern homes and lives, they are succulents.

So gardeners everywhere, frustrated by the constant demands and failures of tropicals, are beginning to rediscover succulents as house plants. And in doing so they are only reaffirming the judgment of their parents and grandparents, who in the twenties and nineties made these plants permanent fixtures in their sunrooms and porches, sitting rooms and kitchens. Even today succulents enjoy a far greater popularity in Europe than in America—a curious fact that is difficult to explain. But a renewed interest in succulents may soon change the style of growing things in American homes.

Succulents as House Plants

We have already suggested why succulents have been traditionally popular as house plants. No other group is so well adapted to the heat, drought, and neglect plants are likely to find indoors. And no other offers such interesting forms and colors, habits and blooms with so little effort and expense. There is no need for special equipment or space—even a crowded window sill can hold a splendid collection. The only real need of succulents indoors is a place in the sun.

Succulents are generally grown indoors before windows, where they are assured of getting most of the available sunlight throughout the day. Alcove windows with glass on three sides are ideal as they greatly increase the amount of available sunlight, and with a little alteration the roof over such windows can sometimes be glassed in too, making a miniature glasshouse. The plants may be placed on a table before the window, on the window sill itself, or on tiered shelves fastened at intervals up the window frame. If these shelves are made of three-eighths-inch plate glass set on metal brackets, they will not only be inconspicuous but interfere very little with the diffusion of light. The lowest shelf, which is set on the sill itself, should be made wider than the rest to accommodate the largest plants. Such a plant window is the ideal arrangement for most rooms as it holds the largest number of plants in the sunniest window with the least effort and expense.

Occasionally succulents are grown in window boxes set on the window sill inside. These can be very satisfactory, as they hold more plants, require less watering, and offer unlimited possibilities for naturalistic planting. But they must be well made, well drained, and not too large, as they must be turned around occasionally to allow the sunlight to reach the plants in front and back evenly. A box five inches wide, five inches deep, and two feet long is about right. Generally speaking, these plant boxes should never be placed outside the windows in summer unprotected. For, with rare exceptions, most succulents acclimated to life indoors would be scorched by the direct sunlight. Of course this sunlight is easily controlled for indoor plants with curtains, venetian blinds, or other forms of shading.

Containers and Potting

Once we have decided where to put our plants we must select their containers and learn how to pot them. Succulents are commonly grown in four kinds of containers: porous clay pots, glazed pots, tin cans, and wooden tubs and boxes. Of these the porous, standard red-clay pots are the most popular and efficient. Because they are deeper than wide, they allow ample room for soil and succulent roots, which are often surprisingly long and vigorous. Because they are porous and have a large hole at the bottom, they promote good drainage and soil aeration. And, finally, they are inexpensive.

But many gardeners find the dull red color and monotonous form of these pots especially unattractive indoors and so prefer using glazed containers. Contrary to some expert opinion, there is no great harm in using glazed pots for succulents provided they have an adequate hole and crockery at the bottom for drainage, and are watered with a little more care to offset the fact that moisture cannot escape from their sides. Actually glazed containers carefully selected with an eye for color and form can become a real asset in setting off the plants and tying in the succulent collection with the décor of the room.

Tin cans and other metal containers are sometimes used for succulents with good results too. In very hot, dry areas they have proved especially good for such relatively moisture-

CACTI AND OTHER SUCCULENTS

A sunny window, two glass shelves, and a remarkable collection prove better than words that succulents can be easy and exciting house plants. On the top shelf, from left to right, are *Euphorbia hermentiana, Kleinia mandraliscae, Adromischus cristatus, Aloe arborescens, Opuntia turpinii,* an opuntia species, and a relative of the yuccas—a dasylirion. On the second shelf are *Opuntia microdasys, Faucaria tigrina*—then skipping the next two figurines—*Chamaecereus silvestrii, Cephalocereus senilis,* and *Lemaireocereus beneckei.* The window sill holds *Euphorbia canariensis, Mammillaria bocasana,* the hybrid *Gasteria beguinii, Hechtia texensis,* and *Gasteria verrucosa.* The table below displays at the rear an agave species, a Stapeliad, *Crassula falcata* in bloom, a haworthia species, and *Ceropegia woodii;* in the foreground a planter with mammillarias and other succulents, a tiny lithops in bloom, *Mammillaria plumosa,* and *Pleiospilos nelii.*

SUCCULENTS IN THE HOME

loving cacti as epiphyllums and echinopses, which sometimes dry out too quickly in more porous containers. Quart, gallon, or five-gallon cans are cleaned, the top cut out, and three or four large drainage holes are punched in the sides of the can at the bottom with a beer-can punch. Then the cans are either dipped inside and out in an asphalt solution or, better still, painted with dark green enamel to prevent rusting. Recently a very attractive commercial nursery can has been developed which has a tapering, fluted bottom that is almost as attractive and easily emptied as a pot. These metal containers are certainly the lightest, most inexpensive, and unbreakable of all but, except for certain moisture-loving species or very large specimens that cannot be potted economically, they are of limited value to the average collector.

We have already mentioned the use of wooden window boxes for succulents, but occasionally other types of wooden tubs, planters, and hanging baskets are used for large specimens in areas where there is difficulty in keeping the plants properly supplied with moisture. These wooden containers are relatively light, inexpensive, and require far less watering than pots or tins, which may be an asset on hot, dry, drafty patios and porches. But they must be well made of durable redwood or cedar, treated with a non-toxic preservative inside, painted or stained outside, and provided with adequate drainage holes.

Far more important than the kind of container we select is the size. Succulents that are underpotted or overpotted not only look unbalanced but grow improperly. It takes a little experience and a handy rule of thumb to select the right pot for each plant. For plants of a rounded form use a pot one inch wider than the diameter of the plant. For tall-growing plants select a pot half as wide as the plant is tall. There will be exceptions to this rule, of course, but succulents generally do best in containers that just fit them with only a little room to spare. Because pots smaller than three inches in diameter are rather difficult to maintain, several very small plants of the same species are better placed in one three- or four-inch pot than in individual thumb pots.

Before the plant is potted, the container should be matched to it, washed and scrubbed free of all dirt and impurities, and the drainage hole enlarged if necessary. A large piece of broken crock is then laid rounded side up over the drainage hole and over this a generous layer of potshards or pea gravel is added for drainage in all pots over four inches in diameter.

The potting soil for succulents should be made up in advance, using equal parts sand, soil, and leaf mold for desert, alpine, and shore line species; and the same with an added part of leaf mold for jungle species. Only clean, coarse river sand must be used in this mixture as fine beach sand packs hard and may contain salt or other impurities. The leaf mold should be well rotted and preferably from hardwood trees such as oak, but any good garden loam will do for the soil. These ingredients should be well mixed and coarsely screened to make a loose, friable, sweet-smelling compost.

Volumes have been written on the subject of soil for succulents. Some "experts" have even suggested making a separate mixture for every species. But actually these plants are remarkably tolerant of any reasonably light, well-drained, porous soil. Growers in very cool, damp regions may wish to add a half part more sand or poultry charcoal or perlite to their compost to make it even lighter and better drained. Others in hot, dry regions may add as much soil and leaf mold to hold moisture. Some growers always add a light sprinkling of hydrated lime, crushed oyster shells, or limestone chips to the soil for any succulents with heavy spines or horny tubercles. Others add a light dusting of bone meal as a safe fertilizer for any mixture. The truth is that any and all of these formulas work, not because they are especially good in themselves but because they all supply the three

HOW TO POT SUCCULENTS

basic needs of succulents: good aeration, steady nourishment, and perfect drainage.

Before being potted, every plant should be carefully examined for pests and diseases. Potted plants are easily turned out of their containers when the soil is slightly damp by holding the pot upside down and rapping the rim on the corner of a table. Plants in cans are removed by cutting the can to the bottom on two sides with tin snips. Once out of their pots, very spiny succulents may be handled with stout leather gloves, rubber-padded coal or ice-cube tongs, or an improvised holder made by rolling several sheets of newspaper into a strap which is placed around the body of the plant with the two free ends serving as a handle. A thorough search should be made of the exposed root ball for scale, mealy bug, and rot. If there is any evidence of pests or disease, the soil should be carefully picked away from the roots, all affected parts cleaned or cut away to the plant body, and the cuts dusted with powdered charcoal or sulfur. If the plants are healthy but have become very root-bound or formed a hard crust at the top of the plant ball, they will be helped if the crust is gently crumbled away and the roots loosened slightly.

The actual process of potting succulents is the same as that used for other plants except for one very important difference. Because these plants are so susceptible to rot from excessive moisture in the soil, especially when their roots have been disturbed or cut, both the plant to be potted and the potting soil must be quite dry at the time of planting and for several days afterwards. A layer of dry soil is laid down over the drainage material in the pot, then the plant is centered over it and more soil added around the plant ball or roots until the pot is half full. To settle this loose soil the pot should be bumped lightly on the potting bench or, if the pot is very large and heavy, the soil may be tamped down with a blunt stick. More soil is then added all around until the roots are buried to exactly the same depth as they were formerly, allowing a reasonable space at the top of the pot for watering. The loose soil is then firmed again by tamping it with a stick, pressing down gently over it with both thumbs, or by bumping the pot on the table.

While these directions will serve to pot most succulents properly, there are many awkward cases that need special treatment. The commonest of these are very tall plants that do not have enough roots to anchor them firmly in the soil. Since these cannot be planted any deeper than they have been growing without danger of rotting, they must be supported until new roots are formed by tying them with raffia or twine to a small stick placed in the pot. Other succulents without roots may sometimes be wedged in place with pieces of broken brick or, if the base of the plant has dried up so that it is concave below, coarse sand may be poured under it to fill the gap until the plant swells and supports itself again. The formation of new roots can be tested by gently moving the plant while the pot is held firmly. A rootless plant will shift slightly when touched, but as roots develop, a definite resistance can be felt until finally the plant becomes quite rigid in the soil.

Unlike other plants, succulents are never watered immediately after potting. The plant and soil are allowed to remain perfectly dry for several days, then they are watered very sparingly for the first month or two. This allows bruised and broken roots to heal which might otherwise rot at once if watered heavily. Some growers like to mulch newly potted succulents with a thin layer of crushed rock or pebbles for appearance's sake, but this can be a dangerous thing as it hides the true condition of the soil beneath and makes watering doubly difficult for the beginner. Another potentially dangerous practice is the use of saucers under the pots to catch excess water. These must be emptied promptly each time the plants are watered or, better still, they may be filled with a layer of pebbles raising the pot out of the water so that

What could be simpler—or more beautiful—than a brass kettle planted with the purple rosettes of *Aeonium arboreum* var. *atropurpureum?*

Any patio or porch will become the center of attraction when decorated with a few succulents. The pots may be of iron, wood, marble, or simple clay. On the top step is a fine specimen of *Opuntia aciculata* in full bloom flanked by the tall, columnar *Lemaireocereus marginatus.* On the second step, in a marble pot, is the ever popular *Kalanchoe tomentosa* and that favorite Prickly Pear, *Opuntia microdasys* var. *rufida.* The tall plant on the lower step left is *Crassula perfoliata,* and the bushy little rosette plant in the center *Aeonium haworthii.*

SUCCULENTS IN THE HOME

the drainage hole is free at all times for proper soil aeration. This and all other phases of maintaining succulents in the home are discussed fully in Chapter Eight.

Dish Gardens

All too often the beginner's first encounter with succulents begins with the purchase or gift of a novelty dish garden from a florist. It may be a little ceramic dachshund or cat or burro, filled with an odd assortment of plants, with a cylindrical cactus growing behind for a tail; or a hollow piece of Cholla wood in which a variety of seedling cacti are decorated with tiny artificial flowers. Whatever it is, it is sure to be hastily planted, overcrowded, and short-lived. The containers seldom have enough soil or provision for drainage, tropical plants and succulents requiring entirely different culture are jammed together indiscriminately, and even the most careful watering and care cannot make them live more than a month or two. All this has given succulents, and more especially dish gardens, a bad name.

Although succulents can be grown in novelty containers without a drainage hole, great care should be taken to fill the bottom one third of such pots with broken crocks and charcoal, to make the soil extremely light and sandy, and to water most sparingly at all times. Actually such containers are not really suitable for succulents, no matter how clever they may be, and anyone interested in growing succulents well should use properly drained containers. There are innumerable shapes and sizes available, and one that is neither too shallow nor too small should be chosen, for a group of succulents planted together need plenty of soil in which to grow. The elegant trays and dishes used by the Japanese for planting their miniature trees, or bonsai, are available at oriental import shops and are not only inexpensive but exquisite in color and form for succulent dish gardens.

Aeonium blooms and rosettes form a striking arrangement here, but even more wonderful is the fact that they will remain beautiful for days—without work or water, without fading or wilting.

SUCCULENTS IN THE HOME

The general method of potting dish gardens is the same as that for potting individual plants; however, greater care must be taken to create a harmonious and beautiful arrangement in the container. If a desert landscape is to be suggested, a few pieces of weathered rock or driftwood carefully chosen for color and texture may be sunk into the soil before planting. With these as a setting small divisions and seedlings of cacti and other succulents may be planted around them artistically. Care should be taken to use plants that require the same general treatment, that contrast nicely in color and texture, and that do not grow too quickly. In the miniature scale of the dish garden the upright stems of a stapelia will suggest a great Organ Cactus, a tiny haworthia becomes a Century Plant, a seedling mammillaria a great Barrel Cactus, and the blue-green tufts of *Sedum dasyphyllum* a bit of desert brush. The possibilities are unlimited.

Of course good taste must always be used to make these living arrangements clean, simple, and uncluttered. Some may wish to add tiny figures and props to the scene, but this generally leads to something less artistic. It is enough to have a handsome dish, one or two well-chosen stones, and a half dozen perfectly spaced plants to create a bit of living desert in the home.

Occasionally succulents are grown in terrariums—glass bowls, aquariums, or brandy snifters partly filled with soil and plants. They are rarely happy in these containers, however, because there is no provision for drainage, the close atmosphere in the bowl induces rot, and the glass cuts off an appreciable amount of sunlight from the plants. The only advantages of such a planting are that it removes spiny plants out of the immediate reach of children, it can go months without watering if fitted with a loose cover, and it does provide a rather dramatic frame for a miniature desert scene. The preparation of such a planting is the same as for a novelty container without drainage, but it requires even closer attention to watering.

CACTI AND OTHER SUCCULENTS

Arrangements

If ever there were plants made to order for the flower arranger, they are succulents. In no other class of arrangement materials can one find such dramatic lines, rich textures, and subtle colors combined with such easy use and incredible lasting qualities. And in no other group can one dispense so completely with the mess and bother of water and bowls, wilted leaves and faded flowers. Succulents are probably the only plants that can be used in an arrangement without water for a month and then planted again without losing a beat. They simply let you have your cake and eat it too.

It would be presumptuous to describe the materials and techniques of flower arrangement here, for any good book on the subject will provide the necessary basic information which can readily be applied to succulents. But it may not be amiss to suggest a few striking ways in which succulents have been used in home decoration. First, of course, there is the traditional arrangement which simply substitutes succulent leaves, stems, or flowers for more commonplace materials. Second, the more difficult composition which combines succulents with stones, driftwood, and other living or dried materials to create a studied contrast of textures and colors. Third, the purely functional arrangement which, for example, sets dozens of small echeverias in a cone of wire mesh to form a miniature Christmas tree, or in a circle of wire to make a lasting holiday wreath, or creates a stunning candleholder of a single large rosette. And, fourth, there is the button garden in which almost any large button is used as a base on which leaves, tip cuttings, or divisions of tiny succulents are fastened with glue or modeling clay to make a long-lasting miniature arrangement.

There is little doubt that as succulents become more widely

A beautiful and lasting holiday centerpiece is created with a few red- and silver-tinted rosettes of echeveria and graptopetalum. The graceful echeveria blooms carry the festive colors behind the candles to complete the picture.

grown they will take an increasingly important place in the field of flower arrangement. Indeed, there is virtually nothing that can be done with other materials that cannot be done with succulents, and much, much more besides.

Corsages

The last but certainly not the least way of using succulents in the home is in making corsages. The same interesting forms, subtle colors, and lasting qualities that make succulents prized plants for arrangements make them ideal materials for corsage work too. It is difficult to imagine more exciting flowers for formal wear than epiphyllums and zygocacti, or more durable subjects for informal wear than tailored clusters of echeveria and sedum. Yet despite their unique beauty and richness these corsages are easily made with the simplest techniques and materials.

The only equipment required is a pair of scissors, wire cutters, florist's wire in several gauges, and a roll of narrow green or brown parafilm stemming tape. The wire should be cut in twelve-inch lengths, using number eighteen wire for the largest flowers and heaviest leaves or rosettes; number twenty-two medium wire for smaller, lighter ones; and number twenty-six fine or number thirty extra-fine wire for the smallest. The lightest possible gauge should be used in every case to reduce the weight of the finished corsage.

The flowers, rosettes, or leaves to be used must be fresh and perfect in all respects and preferably picked in the early morning or just before use. To insure good composition there should be a variety of colors, textures, and sizes ranging from tight buds to mature specimens.

To illustrate the process of making a corsage we might select a small epiphyllum or zygocactus blossom. A length of florist's wire is pushed through the stem of the flower just below the base of the petals until it projects about four inches on the other side. Then the long end is bent down parallel to the stem and the short end carefully bent and wound spirally from the base of the blossom down over the stem and long wire. For very heavy blossoms or rosettes another wire may be inserted in the stem at right angles to the first and wound down similarly. Two or three turns are sufficient to hold the flower firmly, and any excess stem below these turns may be snipped off to lighten the finished corsage. If any length of short wire remains it can be twisted down the long stem wire until it is used up.

To conceal this wiring we take the flower in our left hand and attach and overlap one end of the stemming tape high around the base of the flower. Then with the roll of tape in our right hand the flower is evenly twirled between the fingers and the self-sticking tape automatically feeds off the roll down the stem to the end of the wire. When all the blossoms have been similarly wired and wrapped, they are carefully arranged as they are to appear in the finished corsage and securely wired together. The wire stems can be left as they are, or trimmed evenly and tied with a bow, or wound into curlicues around a pencil or finger and bent back among the blossoms. The technique of wiring single leaves and rosettes, of making bows and other corsage accessories cannot be described in detail here, but any good book on corsage-making will supply the know-how to turn the succulents we grow in our homes into beautiful and lasting floral pieces.

CHAPTER SIX

Succulents in the Garden

While succulents are ideal plants for almost any purpose indoors, they really reach their greatest beauty and usefulness in the garden. And this usefulness is not limited to just those frost-free areas of California, Florida, and the Southwest where they can be grown in the open the year round; but it extends to the North and East, where gardeners have found many new and exciting ways to use succulents out of doors in their summer gardens. Certainly no other plants can bring such colors and textures, such versatility and ruggedness to landscaping. And no others are so easy to grow and maintain out of doors.

The history of succulents in the garden has been a long and checkered one. It probably began with a few adventurous growers who dared to summer their cherished house plants out of doors and found them healthier and more beautiful than ever before. And so they began growing succulents on patios and porches, on walls and in the garden. Then came the elaborate patterned beds of the Victorian era, marvels of industry and imitation. And the hopelessly literal "cactus gardens" of the twenties, which were really geological collections overrun with plants and props.

Now we have our own renascence of interest in succulents,

and for the first time in their long history these plants are being given a more natural, more nearly functional place in the garden. They are being used so freely and intelligently, with such good taste and judgment that there is no doubt succulents are here to stay for all time.

The Rock Garden

The commonest, most natural way to use succulents in the garden is to combine them with stones to make a rock garden. But the modern succulent rock garden is a far cry from the wagon-wheel and skull-littered rock piles of the twenties or the rather austere moraines and screes of the alpine gardener. It is simply a slightly raised, free-form bed in which stones and plants are carefully and sparingly blended together to recreate a miniature desert landscape. It may be as small as three by five feet or it may cover an entire garden, but its principles and techniques are the same.

There are many types of rock garden construction. Some utilize a natural slope in the garden, others the banks of a winding ravine, still others build elaborate terraces and contours. But the easiest and best method for gardeners with a level site is the simple mound—a pile of earth over a central core of drainage material. It requires no excavation, provides perfect drainage, and may be varied in shape and size to fit any location.

This last factor, location, is of utmost importance in making a successful succulent garden. The site selected must be well drained, well ventilated, and relatively frost-free—especially in areas where the plants remain out of doors the year round. An open eastern or southern exposure is generally best. And more important still, the rock garden must fit easily into the landscape picture. It must not be set in the middle of a lawn like a desolate island, or near plants whose colors and textures clash with the strong lines and character of succulents. A place at the edge of the lawn; a bright, secluded

SUCCULENTS IN THE GARDEN

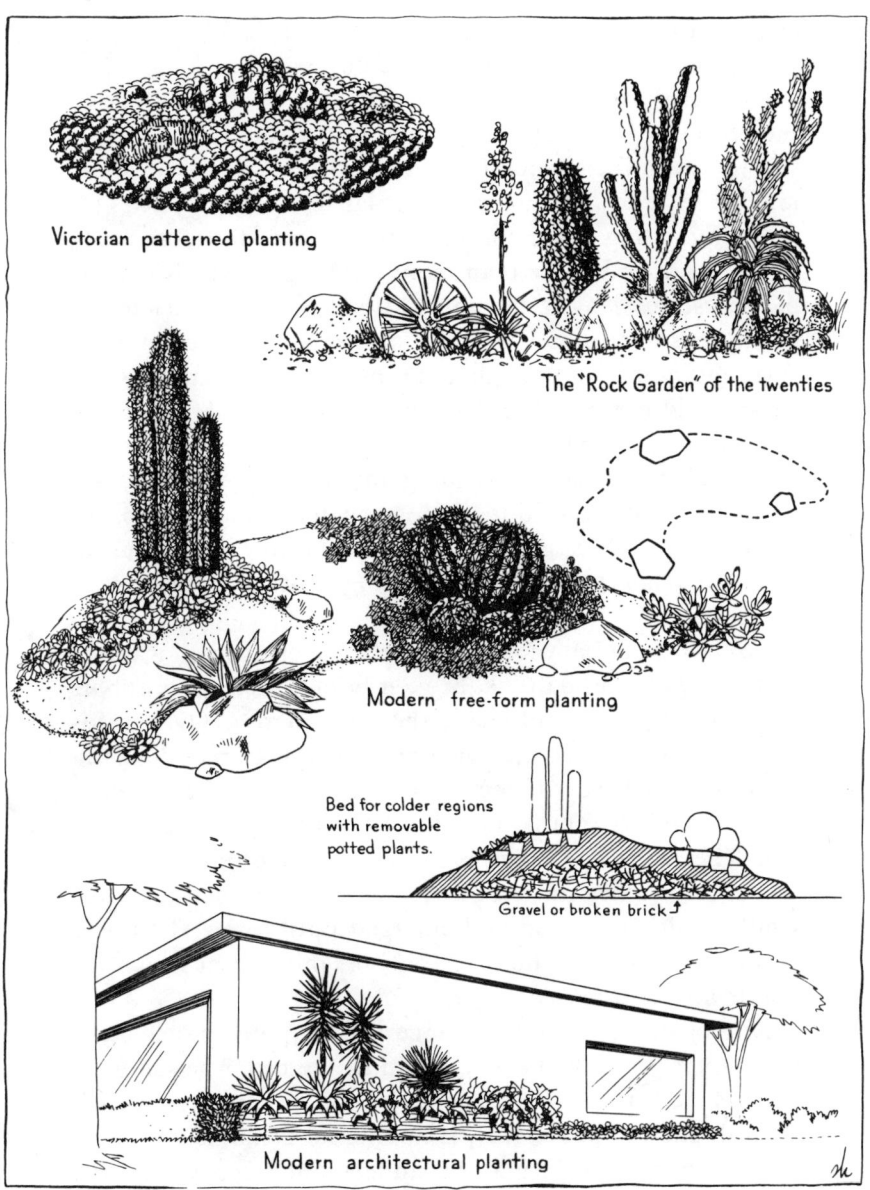

HOW TO PLANT SUCCULENTS

corner of the garden; a spot before a sunny wall—these are good locations for a succulent garden.

Once the proper site has been selected, a rough outline of the proposed bed should be drawn in the soil. Unless necessity forces it, the shape of the rock garden should never be regular. A graceful oval or triangular free-form figure is far more interesting to see and plant, and blends far more easily into the garden picture than more formal patterns. It may be of almost any length, but the width should be restricted to permit easy access for weeding and maintenance from the surrounding paths. Beds that can be reached from only one side should not be more than two or three feet wide; those that can be reached from both sides may be made twice that width. This may seem a trifling matter to the novice, but beds that are difficult to reach not only try tempers and backs but are generally neglected. If wider plantings are planned, some provision for auxiliary steppingstones or paths should be made.

To insure perfect drainage for the succulent bed a three-inch layer of crushed rock, broken brick, or concrete rubble is laid over the ground inside the marked area. Over this is added another three-inch layer of finer materials like pea gravel or potshards. These layers may be shaped roughly as they are laid to approximate the finished appearance of the bed. They may be pushed high in the center and tapered to the edges, gullies and contours may be outlined, and the whole basic form tried and changed until right. Then over this mold is poured the prepared soil mixture in which the plants are to grow.

Any of the soil mixtures suggested for potting succulents in Chapter Five may be used to finish the bed. The soil must be laid at least a foot deep over the entire area—raked, shaped, and tamped evenly. If additional height is desired at the center, more soil may be added, but steep slopes and fussy contours should be avoided as they are unstable and generally wash out with the first heavy watering or rain. Into this carefully prepared mound of soil we now add a few interesting stones to lend weight and texture to the design.

There are many kinds of stones we might use in the succulent garden, but only a few will really do. They must be relatively large, rough and angular in texture, and unobtrusive in color. Weathered limestone is a good choice, and so is tufa, a porous volcanic rock that holds moisture like a sponge and is full of holes that may be planted with tiny sedums and sempervivums. Whatever rock is chosen, it should all be of one kind and character, for there is nothing so ugly and unnatural as a rock garden made of many kinds and colors of stones.

Once the appropriate stones have been chosen, perhaps only three or four to be placed in a bed six by ten feet, the job of fitting them begins. An expert rock gardener might take an hour or two to place them, testing and trying them over and over again until they seem to fall into place as if they belonged. This is a great art, and not easily learned, but the beginner can avoid many mistakes by following a few simple rules. Never place stones on end, but always on their broadest base. Never space them regularly, but always most casually. Never throw stones on the ground, but always bury them at least one fourth their depth in the soil. Never place stratified rocks haphazardly, but always with the strata in one plane. Never use too many small stones, but try to match and fit several of them together to give the appearance of one large rock.

After the stones have been set in place, the whole bed should be thoroughly watered to settle the loose soil and rocks. After a week or ten days, and perhaps another watering, the bed should be given a final shaping before it is planted.

If the rock garden is in one of those relatively frost-free areas in which succulents may be grown out of doors the year

The succulent bed should always be gently sloped and shaped in an interesting free-form pattern. *Dudleya brittonii* is the handsome rosette in the foreground right; the large white clusters beside it are *Echeveria alba* hybrids backed by a solid border of the smaller white rosettes of *Echeveria elegans.* The large cabbage-like plants in the center are *Aeonium nobile,* and behind them a mass of *Kleinia repens* and the taller *Cotyledon teretifolia.*

A few large rocks, carefully placed, enhance any succulent planting. The striking white rosette in the foreground is *Dudleya brittonii;* the large dark plant beside it, *Gasteria carinata;* and the white clusters behind them both, *Echeveria elegans.* To the right of the rock in the center is an aloe, behind it *Kleinia repens* and the tall finger-like *Cotyledon teretifolia* in bloom.

SUCCULENTS IN THE GARDEN

round, the plants are set directly into the soil as any other plants. The soil must be dry, of course, and not watered for a week after planting. But if it is in one of the colder areas where succulents can be put out of doors only briefly in the summer, the potted plants are simply plunged into the bed up to their rims to give the appearance of growing in the soil. Some gardeners in colder regions plant a few hardy cacti—such as *Opuntia phaeacantha, fragilis,* or *rhodantha*—or succulents such as the hardy sedums and sempervivums as permanent fixtures in their rock gardens, to which they add the more tender potted species in summer. Others who never use their rock gardens except for a summer display of potted plants simply substitute coarse sand for the soil mixture usually used to build the mound.

Plants in the rock garden should be carefully arranged according to size, habit, color, and texture. They must never be crowded or planted in regular lines, but in well-spaced drifts with plenty of open ground between. Plants requiring similar treatment or watering are best placed together. Plants requiring shade can be grown beside taller species, near rocks, or in the shade of small-leaved desert trees like the Jerusalem Thorn, *Parkinsonia aculeata,* set in or near the bed. The planting may consist only of cacti, of other succulents, or all combined. Extensive outdoor collections are sometimes planted in a series of free-form beds, each devoted to a single succulent family or tribe. The possibilities and pleasures of rock gardening with succulents are endless.

Patterned Bedding

Sooner or later everyone who admires the wonderful cylindrical forms and rosettes of succulents wishes he might arrange them in a more formal planting, and it is out of such a wish that Victorian gardeners created the very beautiful and intricate art of carpet bedding. In a prominent spot on

CACTI AND OTHER SUCCULENTS

This spectacular mass planting of cacti displays dozens of *Echinocactus grusonii,* the Golden Barrel, blooming in the foreground, and three clusters of tall columnar cacti in the center. They are, from left to right, *Cephalocereus senilis*—with the white hair showing on the four smaller specimens and the taller one, twenty-five feet high, rising out of the picture; *Lemaireocereus marginatus,* just right of the center, with another specimen forty feet high attached to the corner of the house; and the giant Saguaro, *Carnegiea gigantea,* the thick column at the right supported by a pipe. The two dark treelike plants in the background, at the extreme right and left, are *Euphorbia ingens,* and the smaller tree below the balcony a cereus.

SUCCULENTS IN THE GARDEN

the front or back lawn of great country estates a large planting bed was prepared, just as we have described for the rock garden but without stones and perfectly regular in form. On this round, oval, oblong, or square planting area various designs were drawn with a stick and outlined with sand. The patterns could be abstract, or represent birds or animals, or actually copy the design of a Turkish carpet in the great house. When the planning was finished, the various areas were planted with dwarf plants and flowers carefully chosen to re-create the colors and textures of the original model.

It is easy to see why the tiny, slow-growing globular and cylindrical cacti and the prim rosettes of other succulents were favorites for this kind of work. They could be planted close together without fear of rank growth, they required far less care than other plants, and the rich colors of their spines and leaves remained the same throughout the season. Beginning with a few larger Barrel Cacti in the middle, the design was carefully worked out with varicolored mammillarias and echinopses, astrophytums and lobivias, echeverias and sedums. Of course a tremendous number of plants were required, all of uniform size and quality, and a large reserve to replace any that might fail. But more important still, this type of bedding required great skill and good taste.

The day of patterned bedding is by no means over. It can still be wonderfully effective if the home gardener wishes to devote the time and thought necessary to create these living pictures in the garden. In mild climates they can be a permanent fixture, in colder areas plants may either be set with their pots or planted out and lifted each season.

Wall and Ground-Cover Plantings

A much more practical use for succulents is in wall and ground-cover plantings. Wall gardens are becoming increasingly popular in many parts of the country where dry-wall

More and more, succulents are leaving the rock garden and desert planting to move into the perennial border and informal flower bed. Here succulents combine happily with perennials and shrubs to form a neat, colorful, carefree border. The tall rosettes against the fence are *Aeonium urbicum* and the smaller, branched rosettes at the corner are *Aeonium arboreum.* In front of them, at the extreme left, are three large, low rosettes of *Aeonium canariense;* behind the pinks, in the center of the picture, is *Sedum pachyphyllum;* and beside it the spotted *Aloe zebrina* in bloom with the lower, dark green rosettes of *Aloe mitriformis* hybrids on either side. The tall, finger-like gray plants beside the aloes are *Kleinia tomentosa* and the shorter ones a dudleya species. In the foreground are, among other things, a variety of sedums and hybrid echeverias ending, just above the far right corner, with the silver Ghost Plant, *Graptopetalum paraguayense.*

SUCCULENTS IN THE GARDEN

construction is used to retain steep banks and fills. These walls are easily made by laying successive layers of rocks, without mortar, against the exposed grade. In very cold areas a concrete foundation is sometimes required extending below the frost line, but generally the wall may be built on the bare ground.

The first course of the wall is made with the largest rocks, laid on their broadest side and selected with some attention to strata, colors, and fit. Over, around, and behind this first row good garden soil is tamped down firmly. Before the gardener proceeds with the next course, the plants should be laid on the soil with their roots spread into the depths of the wall and covered with more soil. To prevent succeeding layers of rock from squeezing down too hard on these roots a wedge of stone should be inserted to hold each course of rocks slightly apart. The same process is repeated with each layer—filling in soil, planting, and wedging—each successive course being slightly recessed from the one below and slightly tilted up to catch the maximum sunlight and rain and provide quick drainage.

Good subjects for planting in cold areas are the hardy sedums and sempervivums. In frost-free areas almost any succulents suitable for growing in this manner will do. It must not be assumed that only new walls can be planted. Crevices in old walls may also be packed with soil and planted, but it is a difficult and exasperating job, and the plants rarely thrive as well. There are no special rules for arranging plants in a wall, but good judgment should be used not to plant a rampant grower above a delicate species, or to use plants which look uneasy when grown on the perpendicular.

A still more important use of succulents in mild-winter climates is for ground covers. Thousands of homes in California and the Southwest have used the trailing mesembryanthemums and other succulents as lawn substitutes, as parkway plantings, and as retainers for embankments and fills.

Succulents are perfect plants for banks and ground covers, terraces and rock walls. Here *Cotyledon barbeyi* grows out of pockets in a stone wall, with the silvery-white *Kleinia tomentosa* cascading down from above.

SUCCULENTS IN THE GARDEN

Hundreds of miles of state highways and freeways are planted with succulents to make them more beautiful and to prevent erosion. Even in colder climates the hardy sedums have long been used as ground covers in landscaping. There are certainly no easier or more colorful plants for this purpose, and none that are so quickly and inexpensively installed. The only real shortcomings of succulents as ground covers are that they cannot stand foot traffic, they sometimes become leggy and coarse and require severe thinning, and they are generally tender. But to offset this they can be propagated in unlimited quantities by cuttings, they are practically sun- and drought-proof, and they thrive where few other plants can succeed.

Espaliers, Planters, and Baskets

Of the many new uses to which succulents have been put in recent years, none is so exciting and promising as their use in architectural plantings. If ever there were plants expressly made for our modern homes and gardens, patios and lanais, they are succulents. In line, color, and texture they jibe perfectly with the clean, spacious spirit of modern housing. So it is no surprise to find them used in increasing numbers and ways to complement our new architecture and way of life.

Perhaps one of the most striking uses of succulents today is as espaliers on broad wall surfaces. Many of the climbing and trailing species can be used, but especial favorites are the spectacular epiphyllums and night-blooming cacti. These are either planted in beds at the foot of the wall or placed in large tubs or boxes in front of the area to be covered. Then the long, pliant branches are carefully trained and tied to a permanent trellis of wood placed in the tub or bed, or to a grid of wires attached to the wall. Formal, geometric espalier patterns are not always possible with succulents, but the gracefully scalloped branches of the epiphyllums and the

Many succulents make beautiful and easy-to-care-for hanging-basket plants, and one of the finest is the Burro's Tail, *Sedum morganianum,* shown here. The ground planting below consists chiefly of aeoniums on the left and gasterias on the right.

SUCCULENTS IN THE GARDEN

slender, snakelike stems of the night-blooming cacti have a rhythm and pattern all their own. And when the wall bursts into bloom, the effect is unbelievable.

Equally popular is the current practice of using succulents in special raised planters, either built against the house or in a patio, deck, or special garden area. These architectural planters are of many styles and sizes. They may be nothing more than a raised brick planting bed, a very large box made of weathered redwood, or a huge ceramic or metal bowl. But in them are planted a variety of succulents and other popular drought-resistant plants such as yuccas, dasylirions, nolinas, beaucarneas, puyas, hechtias, and dyckias. These planters are, of course, as carefully prepared with drainage and soil as any other container or bed, and given protection from frost when necessary. They are in many ways the perfect answer for the gardener who wishes an unusual modern planting with little expense or maintenance.

The last way of using succulents in the garden is as hanging-basket plants. There are many species that can be shown off to better advantage with this method of growing than with any other—such as some of the climbing and tree-dwelling cacti, the trailing crassulas, sedums, and mesembryanthemums. All these and many more have been treasured as hanging-basket plants for generations, and they still have a place in every collection. They may be planted in hanging clay pots, tubs, tins, or moss-filled wire baskets. All are satisfactory, although the more porous containers dry out very rapidly and must be watered with great care. They should all be fitted with ample drainage material and given a slightly richer, heavier soil to offset the rapid loss of moisture and plant foods because of their suspended position. The wire baskets—heavily lined with two inches or more of damp florist's sheet moss—are especially good for epiphyllums and other tree-dwelling species, but they are the most difficult to maintain. In semitropical regions these tree-dwelling succulents are sometimes also grown in a thick slab of florist's moss attached with poultry netting and staples to the trunk or branches of high-branching trees such as oak, olive, or elm. The bare-root plants are securely wired against this cushion of moss and grow into it without any soil or care except occasional watering just as they would in their native habitat.

A few well-grown basket specimens hanging at eye level are elegant fixtures for any patio or porch, lath house or greenhouse. The additional work involved in keeping them is slight when compared with the graceful line of their stems and branches, the subtle colors and textures of their leaves, and the brilliant display of their flowers. No collection should be without them.

CHAPTER SEVEN

Collecting, Buying, and Propagating

Now that we have surveyed the evolution of succulents, their major families, and some of the ways we can use them in our homes and gardens, it is time to think of our own collections. And certainly what the novice needs at this point is a little plain down-to-earth advice from someone who has nothing to buy or sell, who has survived a great enthusiasm for these plants and emerged neither disgusted with succulents nor a fanatic, someone who knows that honest advice is the hardest thing to give—or take—in the world.

"The only thing to do with good advice is to pass it on," wrote Oscar Wilde. "It is never of any use to oneself." Looking back over many years of growing succulents, I am encouraged to set down here a few bits of advice learned at great expense but, unfortunately, too late to use myself.

Collecting

The first problem in growing succulents is knowing and selecting the best varieties. How I wish someone had helped me as I pored over the catalogues, wandered through the nurseries, stood bewildered at the shows in those days gone by. Every glowing description I read tempted me, for it never occurred to me that all those varieties could not possibly be the "biggest," the "best," the "showiest." When buying plants I always assumed the higher-priced varieties were best, not knowing price was determined only by scarcity, not worth. At flower shows I fell in love with individual plants and blooms, never knowing how they would grow for me or how I would use them. As a result I ended up with more varieties than I wanted or could care for, a sizable hole in my bank roll, and an ever growing headache.

When it was all over, I discovered there were some succulents in every family that were outstanding. They had everything an ideal succulent must have: vigor, good color and form, abundant and attractive bloom, and easy propagation. I have tried to indicate some of these choice plants in my survey in Chapters Three and Four. Of course there are many who will disagree with my selections. Let me say that they are based first on my personal experience and tastes, and second on the desire to have the finest succulent plants and blooms the year round with a minimum of cost and effort. I realize each grower will wish to amend these lists to suit his own experiences, growing conditions, and tastes. But the beginner cannot go wrong starting his collection with some of these varieties or, indeed, ending with them, as I did.

No doubt the reader has already discovered some plants here that seem especially interesting and exciting. He might well begin his collection with them, and as his interest and experience grow he will find some particular family or genus so irresistible that he will soon become a specialist. The succulent hobby is virulent and contagious, and there is no cure for it except more plants, more books, more information. The collector should read all the literature available on succulents in general and his specialty in particular. A good basic list is suggested in Chapter Ten. He should visit cactus-succulent nurseries at every opportunity and study their catalogues carefully. He should see great desert plant collections like the fifteen-acre display at the Huntington Botanical Gardens in San Marino, California, near Los Angeles; or at the Missouri Botanical Gardens in St. Louis. He should join the Cactus and Succulent Society of America, P.O. Box 3010, Santa Barbara, CA 93130, or inquire there for the name of a cactus-succulent club in his own locality. In all these ways he will find the succulents he wants to grow and the information he needs to grow them successfully.

Buying

Once the beginner has decided what succulents he wants, another problem faces him: How can he know and find the best possible plants of those varieties? Buying succulents wisely is an important technique that most amateurs learn only after much needless expense and disappointment. Yet, actually, anyone can become a good buyer by learning a few simple rules.

Always buy from a reputable nurseryman, preferably a succulent specialist—never from supermarkets, ten-cent stores, or department stores. These stores often receive good plants from reputable growers, but they seldom have the proper conditions or help to keep them correctly labeled and growing until they are sold. "Bargain" plants are usually expensive at any price. Unscrupulous promoters sometimes offer large plants collected in the desert at very low prices, but these specimens are usually impossible to re-establish, and such wasteful destruction of native plants is strictly forbidden by law in several states and should not be encouraged. In any event, there is no particular advantage in buying large-specimen plants. For the strong container-grown seedlings and cuttings offered by most nurserymen are actually a better buy for the beginner. These plants are very inexpensive, easily transplanted, and become established so quickly that they often overtake the larger plants in a few years.

It is always desirable to select your plants personally, if possible, although it is perfectly safe to order by phone or mail from established firms. In selecting any plant judge it against other plants of the same variety and size in the nursery. Succulents vary greatly in growth habit and appearance according to species and variety. Some are naturally lanky, sparse-leaved, dwarf, bushy, or strong. Pick the most normal plant—not the tallest or the most heavily budded or the biggest—but the one which is well formed from the ground up, with the freshest color and the best shape. Actually if you select the plant with the greatest number of healthy leaves or branches you will probably have the plant with the best root system too, for the quantity and quality of foliage and stems are a very good indication of the quantity and quality of the roots in the container below. The plant must be absolutely free of any insect pests or diseases. Examine the stems and foliage of the plant carefully for scale or mealy bug, which can invade even the best-regulated nurseries occasionally. But when all is said and done, your best guide and insurance in buying succulents will always be to patronize a reliable professional grower.

Propagating

Although most of our plants may be acquired from nurserymen, there is a great deal of interest and enjoyment in learning how to propagate succulents for oneself. Sooner or later every collector wants to swap cuttings and seeds with other enthusiasts, wants to grow rare or difficult species that cannot be bought, wants to multiply choice plants or even improve them by hybridization. Fortunately he can do all these things and more with very little effort or equipment, for succulents are among the easiest of all plants to propagate. The best means of propagating each genus and species has already been suggested in Chapters Three and Four.

COLLECTING, BUYING, AND PROPAGATING

Seeds. One of the most satisfactory methods of propagating succulents, though perhaps the slowest, is by seed. This is the method used by most commercial growers because plants raised from seed are generally lower in cost, healthier, more perfectly formed, and more easily acclimated than plants raised by other means or collected in the wild. Some succulents cannot be raised in any other way. Others set seed so rarely, grow so slowly, or self-hybridize so freely that propagation by seed is impractical. For the amateur, who can buy almost any succulent seedling from a nurseryman for a few cents, this method is generally far more trouble than it is worth. But for raising large quantities of plants cheaply or just for fun, for growing very rare plants otherwise unobtainable or developing new hybrids, it is well worth knowing.

The amateur need not concern himself too much with the intricacies of hybridization, for he can usually buy good seed from succulent dealers or collect the seed formed on his own plants. But he should understand the process of fertilization, which is the beginning of all propagation by seed. In a cactus flower, for example, the long, thick organ which protrudes from the very center is called the *pistil.* It is the female organ and consists of three parts: a swollen base called an *ovary,* a long stemlike part called a *style,* and at the top of the style several branches which spread out like a star and are called the *stigma.* Around this pistil are a number of slender, threadlike organs called *stamens.* These are the male organs and consist of a threadlike stalk called a *filament,* which is topped by a little organ called an *anther,* which contains the yellow dust called *pollen.* When the flower is mature, the stigma opens wide and becomes moist and sticky. Any pollen grains which chance to fall or be rubbed on this surface are stimulated by the moist secretion and emit tubes which grow down the whole length of the style, below the flower, into the ovary, where they unite with the ovules. As soon as the pollen tube enters the ovule, fertilization takes place and the ovule quickly becomes a seed.

In the process called hybridizing, this natural fertilization is strictly controlled. When the flower is half formed, some of the petals and sepals are cut away with cuticle scissors, and through this opening all the filaments are eased out and their anthers cut off to prevent chance pollination. The flower is then covered with a bag large enough to permit it to open fully. In a few days when the flower is mature and the stigma is expanded and moist, pollen from another species is gathered on a clean camel's-hair brush and applied to the receptive stigma. The flower is then quickly bagged again, tied securely at the bottom, and labeled with the date and name of both parents. The process of fertilization then takes place as usual, except now we know both parents in the union and can predict the offspring quite accurately by Mendel's law.

Very soon after fertilization takes place the ovary begins to swell and the fruit is formed. If it is a dry capsule it will split when ripe to release its seeds, and so must be bagged or gathered just before that time. If it is a pulpy fruit, like the cactus, the seeds are removed when the fruit is ripe and soft by squashing the pulp in a bowl of water. After the seeds are washed well, the water is strained off and they are spread on a newspaper to dry. After drying, the seeds can be cleaned further by rubbing them together gently to remove any dried pulp still on them. The clean seeds should then be stored in a cool, dry, well-ventilated place until time for planting.

The best time to start most succulent seeds is in spring or early summer. The warmer weather and good growing conditions at that time of year insure quick results and allow the seedlings to become well established before winter. Most succulents require a bottom heat of 70°F. or more for optimum germination, especially at night. If one does not have access to a greenhouse, hotbed, or naturally heated room, a wooden box about a foot deep may be fitted with a 25-watt electric

COLLECTING, BUYING, AND PROPAGATING

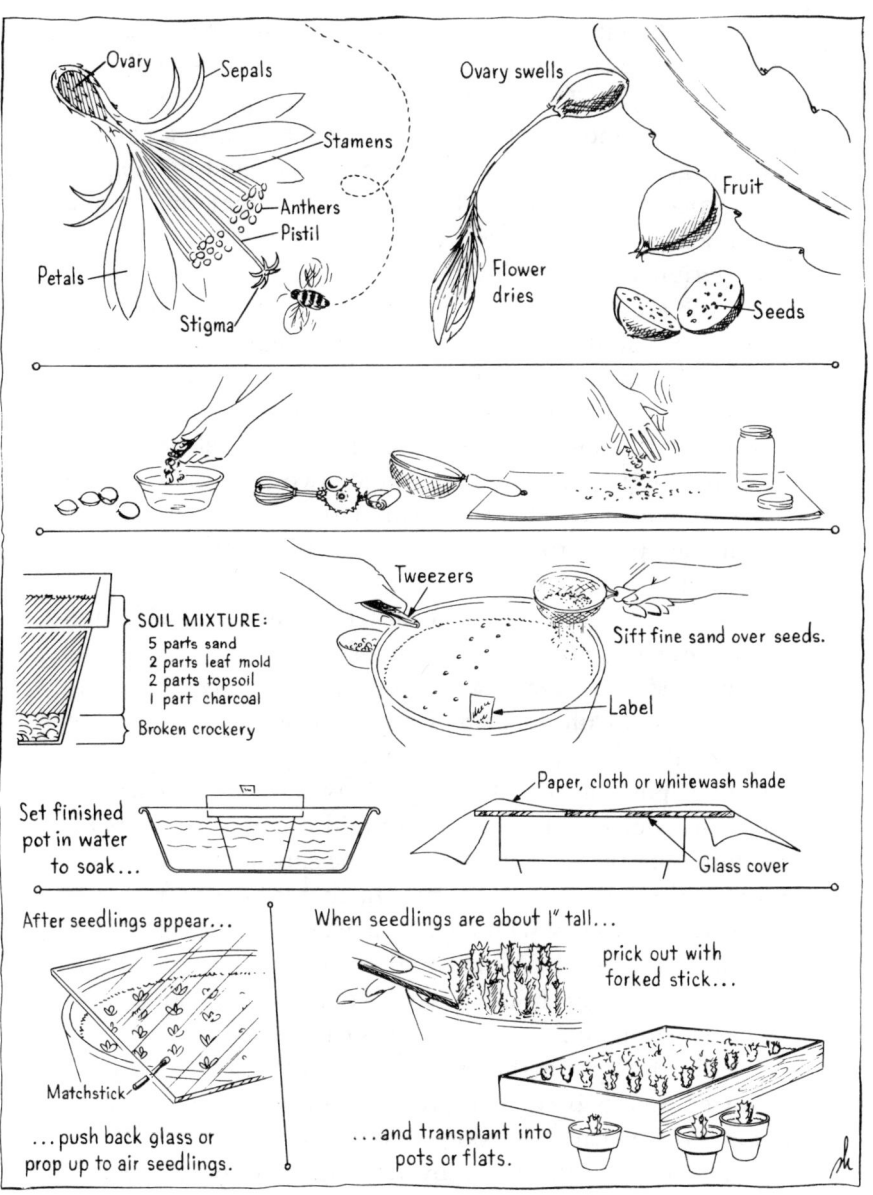

HOW TO GROW SUCCULENTS FROM SEED

light placed on its side at the bottom, and six inches over that a floor of open slats or strong wire mesh should be built. On this false floor, well above the light, the seed pots are set in a pan of damp sand, and the whole box covered with a pane of window glass. With a little experimentation and the help of an inexpensive thermostat to regulate the light this simple propagating box will work wonders.

To germinate only a few succulent seeds the best containers to use are squat, four-inch, red-clay fern pots, although other types will do. They should be thoroughly scrubbed before using and sterilized with boiling water if necessary. In the bottom of each the usual drainage material is arranged, and over this a soil mixture made of five parts clean, coarse sand; two parts well-rotted leaf mold; two parts topsoil; and one part powdered charcoal. This compost should be well mixed and put through a quarter-inch screen to make a loose, well-drained seed bed. The pot should be rapped lightly on a bench to settle the soil and the surface leveled and pressed down gently with a block of wood.

If the seeds are large they may be placed evenly on the surface of the soil with the help of a pair of tweezers. If they are very fine they should simply be dusted lightly over the surface. One pot may be planted with two or more species if small strips of wood or metal are laid down as dividers on the soil. But the seed must never be sown too thickly or mixed indiscriminately in the pot. Each pot or section should be labeled separately with a small plastic label giving the botanical name, approximate number of seeds sown, and the date. Then the seed should be covered no deeper than its own height by sifting fine, clean sand over it evenly.

The finished pot is then set in a pan of tepid water up to its lower rim to become thoroughly saturated by capillary action. And when it is completely soaked it should be removed from the water and allowed to drain completely before taking its place on the greenhouse bench, in the hotbed, or

COLLECTING, BUYING, AND PROPAGATING

propagating box. No matter where it stands, a pane of glass should be put over the pot to conserve moisture and prevent excessive evaporation. If the glass sweats profusely it may be removed and wiped dry occasionally. If there are signs of fungus or algae on the soil, a light spraying of Semesan or other fungicide may be used.

Germination varies among succulents from one day for some of the Stapeliads to as long as a year or more for certain difficult cacti. The average is probably two or three weeks. Germination is affected by many factors—soil moisture and temperature, the season and climate, and the freshness or age of seeds. Some succulent seeds are expressly designed by nature to resist germination for many months or even years to coincide with the availability of moisture in their native habitat. Most desert plants produce their seeds at the end of a rainy season which is followed by a long drought. So if the seeds germinate at once they are quickly burned up. To prevent this nature has coated them, just as a pharmacist coats delayed-action pills, with a thick, hard, or waxy coating that must be softened or worn off with just the right amount of moisture, just the right amount of abrasion and swelling before they will germinate. This explains why fresh seeds so often lie for months in the soil before germinating, while older seeds germinate at once. The gardener who would grow succulents from seed must have both knowledge of and patience for such things.

Once the seed is germinated the glass cover should be lightly shaded with a piece of cheesecloth or waxed paper. This admits light but prevents the direct rays of the sun from burning the tender seedlings. When all the seeds have germinated, the pot should be ventilated for a few hours daily by pushing the glass back a little or by propping it up from the pot rim with a matchstick. Too much air and light at once will cause the seedlings to become red or bronze in color and burn, too little favors the growth of algae on the soil and rotting of the plants. But as the seedlings develop, more and more air and light can be given until the glass is removed entirely. The soil should be kept reasonably damp throughout the germination and "hardening-off" period by occasionally immersing the pot up to its lower rim in a pan of tepid water. After the glass is removed and the seedlings begin to show their characteristic leaves or growth, watering can be lessened somewhat but never neglected.

The young seedling plants should be grown on in the same pot through the winter and into the following spring. Then they are carefully transplanted to new pots or flats, using the same soil mixture as for the seed bed but with four parts of leaf mold instead of two. The tiny plants must be handled very gently, either with tweezers or at the end of a wooden plant label which has a forklike V notch cut into it. They should be generously spaced, lightly firmed in, and watered thoroughly from below. They will grow rapidly in the new soil and should be transplanted into other pots or flats as often as they become crowded, which may be two or three times a year. When they are large enough to fit a three-inch pot, they should be potted individually in one of the soil mixtures recommended in Chapter Five and grown on as any other potted succulent.

Cuttings. The simplest and certainly the most popular method of propagating succulents is by cuttings. Unlike seeds, which sometimes take several years to make mature flowering plants and then may or may not be true to the species from which they were taken, cuttings often make sizable blooming plants in a few months and are always true to type. They require no special equipment or tedious waiting, no special care or delicate handling. Of all plants succulents are probably the quickest and easiest to grow from cuttings.

The best time to take succulent cuttings is in spring or summer, just as the plants come out of their resting season

COLLECTING, BUYING, AND PROPAGATING

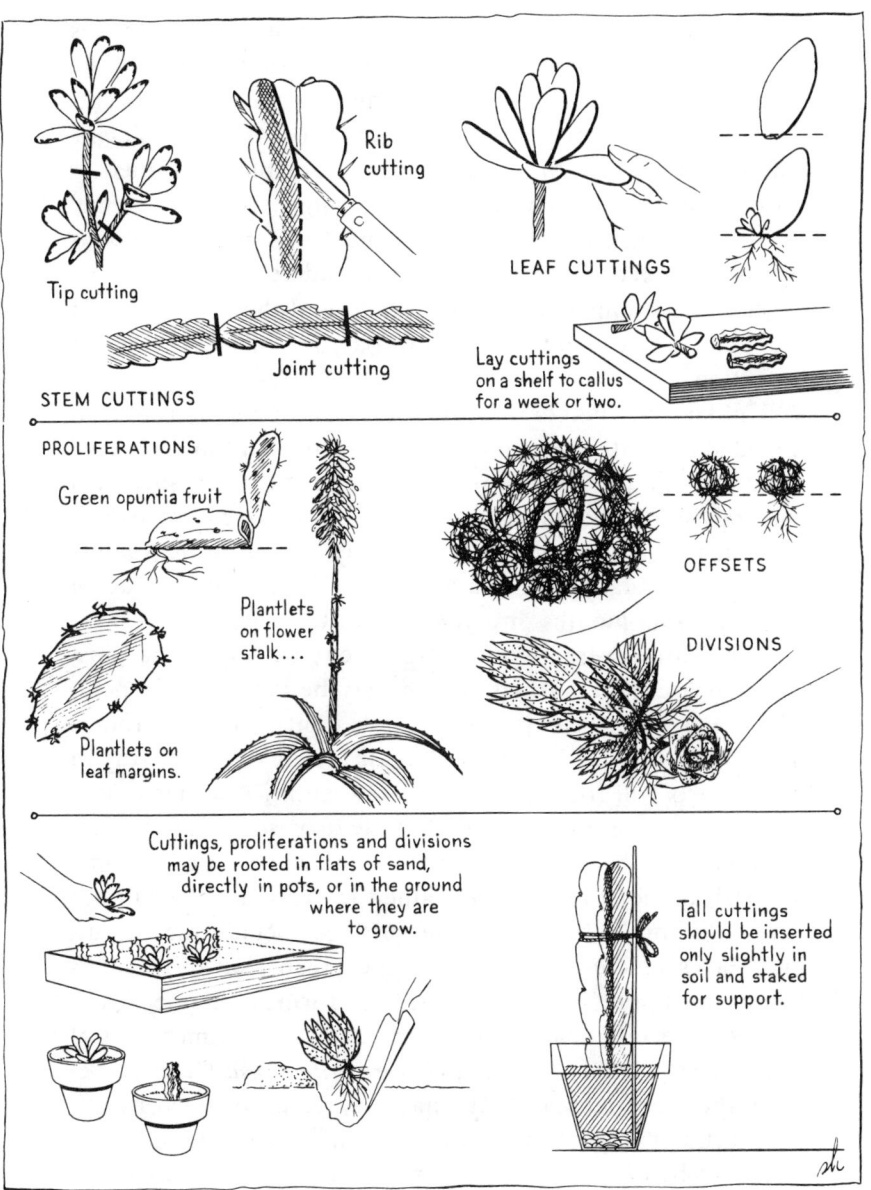

HOW TO MAKE CUTTINGS AND DIVISIONS

and begin to grow vigorously. Plump, healthy leaves or stems should be chosen, preferably from the mature growth of the previous season. They should be fairly large, as sizable cuttings make stronger plants and bloom more quickly. All cuts should be made with a sharp knife, razor blade, clipper, or saw, depending on the size of the cuttings, and never simply broken or torn from the parent plant. Cuts on large outdoor plants an inch or more in diameter should be made diagonally so that the stump will not hold water, and the wound should be dusted with powdered charcoal or sulfur to prevent infection.

Unlike other plants that wilt easily and must be rooted at once, succulents are practically wilt-proof and must indeed be dried out a bit before rooting lest they rot. All succulent cuttings should be put on a cool, shady, well-ventilated shelf to callus for a week or two before they are put in the rooting medium. Actually very heavy cuttings may be dried out for as long as six months or a year without ill effects.

There are several types of succulent cuttings. The most popular are stem cuttings, which may be taken at any point along the stem, near the tip, at the joints, or even from a portion of the stem, such as a single rib or tubercle. Any of these parts will root and make a new plant. Another type is the leaf cutting, in which a whole leaf or sometimes a part of a leaf may be put to root just as one roots a Rex begonia or African violet leaf. Closely allied to these are the cuttings known as proliferations. These cuttings include the sprouting leaves of the bryophyllums; the green fruit of opuntias which root; the bulbils or plantlets formed on the flower stalks of certain agaves, aloes, haworthias, and members of the Crassula family such as *Echeveria gibbiflora.* Here too belong the multitude of plants that may be propagated by offsets, little plantlets formed around a mother plant, and those that can be propagated by simply dividing a matted clump. All of these—leaves, plantlets, flower stalks, offsets, and divisions—require much the same treatment as stem cuttings, for whatever roots some of them may have will either be broken and die back, be severely shocked, or cut off in the process of removal and preparation for planting.

After being severed from the parent plant, preferably at a joint to make the smallest wound possible, and having been dried, these cuttings may either be rerooted in individual pots just as if they were established plants, planted out in the ground where they are to grow, or rooted in flats or pots of coarse sand. Generally most gardeners like to root their cuttings in sand first, before potting or planting them. The rooting medium must be several inches deep, well drained, and a little on the dry side. The cured cuttings are inserted only deep enough to stand firmly in the sand. Deep planting is to be avoided at all costs as it quickly leads to rot. Tall cuttings should be tied to a small stake for support, and easily rotted plants such as the euphorbias or those with very large cut surfaces should not be buried at all, but simply laid on the sand or held over it supported by a stake. The cuttings should be placed in a warm, half-shaded spot and watered very sparingly until fresh color and plumpness or new growth show that roots have been formed. Then the plants are lifted and potted or transplanted as any other succulents.

Grafts. The last and least used method of propagating succulents is grafting, a process of bringing together the growing cells of two related plants to make them unite and grow as one. In this process a stem cutting, called a *scion,* instead of being placed in sand to form its own roots, is united with the root system of another plant, called the *understock.* The added impetus of the older, more vigorous root system of the understock forces the rare or weak scion to prodigious growth, permits seedlings to be matured more quickly, preserves strange crests and monstrosities that are often difficult to root, and allows the propagator to form weeping treelike standards and novelties that lend interest to any collection. But unfortunately not all succulents can be grafted, only those that have a definite cambium, or growth layer, in their stems, the dicotyledons, and of these only plants belonging to the same family. So of the major plant families we have surveyed only members of the Cactus, Euphorbia, and Milkweed families can be grafted. We have suggested some of the possibilities, methods, and species to be used for understocks and scions in these families in Chapters Three and Four.

There are four methods of grafting commonly used for succulents. The first is called a flat graft, and consists simply of fitting a scion cut with a flat base to an understock cut with a flat top. The second method is called a cleft graft, because it fits a scion cut with a wedge-shaped base into a V cleft in the understock. The third method is called a side graft, because both stock and scion are prepared with long, slanting cuts that fit exactly when joined. And last is the stab graft, which is so named because a deep upward stab is made in the understock into which a scion is wedged end up. Each of these methods has its own uses and advantages. The flat graft, which is easiest of all, is used especially for thick, globular scions; the cleft and side grafts for slender scions; and the stab graft for flat, trailing species.

The one imperative in grafting is that the stock and scion must be of the same family and as closely related within that family as possible. In the Cactus family, for example, the small and difficult tephrocacti, epiphyllums, and rhipsales are commonly grafted on the spineless platyopuntias or *O. subulata;* the small globular and slender cylindrical *Cereeae* on understocks such as *Nyctocereus serpentinus* or *Selenicereus macdonaldiae;* and the larger globular or cylindrical species on stocks such as *Trichocereus spachianus* or *Cereus peruvianus.* The list is endless, and always open to argument and experimentation. But whatever grafting stock is used it must always be large and vigorous enough to support the scion, not only at the time of grafting but when the graft reaches

COLLECTING, BUYING, AND PROPAGATING

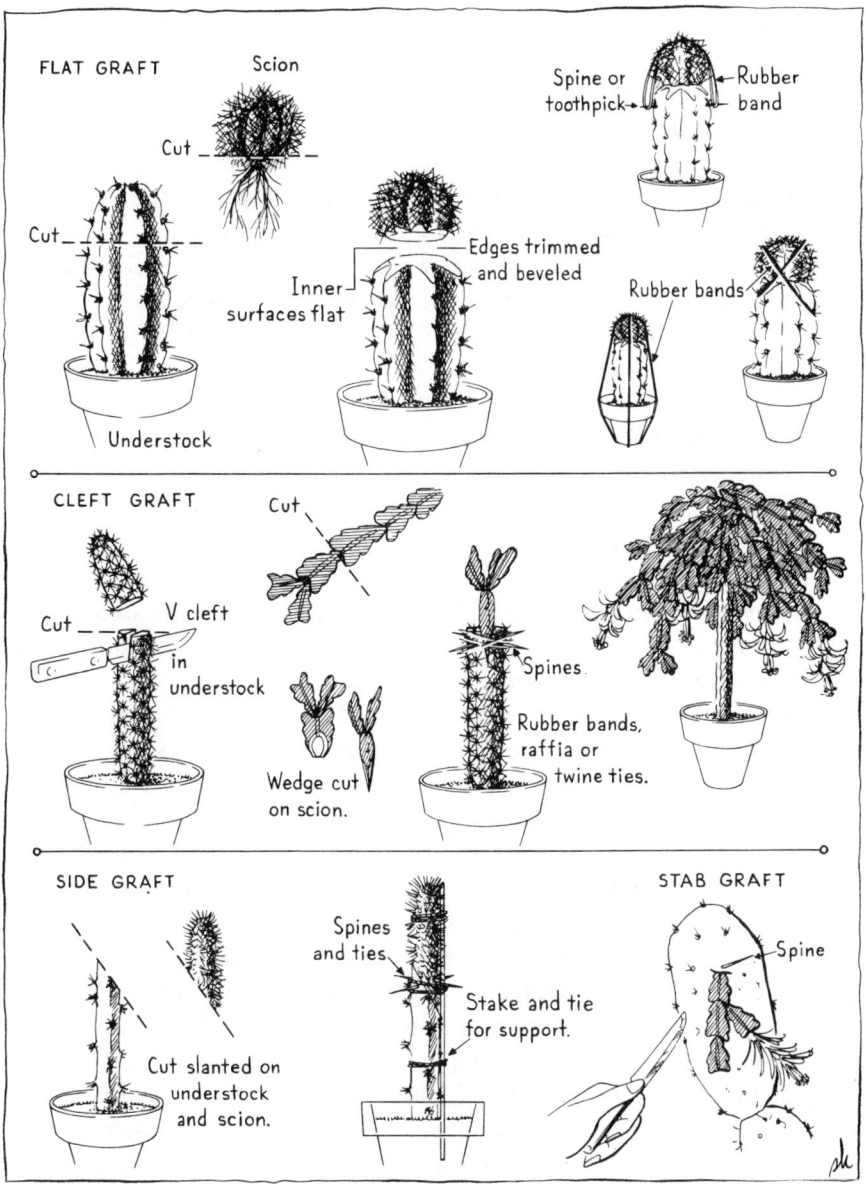

HOW TO GRAFT

normal size. The rule that the stock must be at least ten times the weight of the scion is a good one. It may or may not be rooted at the time of grafting, as in an emergency succulents are sometimes grafted first and then the understock is rooted. But this is neither customary nor desirable, even though succulents can be united and remain alive without roots for some time. The scions should always be plump and fresh and taken from the firm growing tips or new offshoots of healthy plants. They may be equal to the understock in diameter or very much smaller, but they must never be larger.

The understock should always be cut just slightly above the last complete cycle of growth, where the stem feels firm but is neither entirely mature and hard nor watery and soft. A tall stock may be used to form a standard for a trailing variety or to better display an unusual scion and keep it out of dirt and moisture, or a short one grafted only an inch or two above the ground so that as the scion grows the understock will be hidden completely and the plant will seem to be growing on its own roots. Both types have their advantages and disadvantages, but in the last analysis it should be understood that grafting is not a permanent way of growing succulents. Although many grafts last for years, grafting is essentially a way to speed propagation and grow plants to a size where they can continue on their own roots. Many growers cut off scions at the union when they have reached the desired size and root them because they feel the plants are more valuable, attractive, and permanent on their own roots.

The equipment needed for grafting is extremely simple and easily assembled. A pair of clippers or a small keyhole saw to cut heavy stocks and scions; razor blades and a thin, sharp knife to trim them perfectly; leather gloves or tongs to handle very spiny specimens; a supply of soft rubber bands in assorted lengths; long, slender opuntia spines or toothpicks to fasten the grafts or hold the rubber bands; soft raffia or twine for

COLLECTING, BUYING, AND PROPAGATING

tying; and a few paper bags to cover outdoor grafts complete the list.

The best time for grafting is spring or summer, when both stocks and scions are in good growing condition. It is possible to graft at other seasons, especially to save a rare scion, but more care is needed and the results will not be as quick. Once the plants and method of grafting have been selected, the stock and scion should be cut and trimmed to fit as closely as possible. The edges of the stock and scion in flat grafts are usually beveled to cut away interfering spines and more nearly match the surface diameters of the two parts. Success depends in a very large measure on fitting the cut surfaces evenly so that the cambium, or growth layers, of both parts are in contact over as much area as possible. The cuts must be kept absolutely free of all dirt, dust, or foreign matter. If the parts bleed so profusely that the sap threatens to interfere with the union, they may be soaked in water for a few minutes to dissolve the sap, and any excess may be scraped away gently just before the parts are brought together.

The stock and scion should be joined quickly, evenly, and firmly, and the union held in place with one or another of the following devices. For holding flat grafts the best method is to pass rubber bands under the pot and over the scion on two sides; to attach one rubber band to a strong opuntia spine or toothpick inserted in one side of the understock and run it over the scion to another spine or toothpick inserted on the other side; or if the understock has long, downward-pointing spines, the ends of two rubber bands may be hooked on them as they cross over the top of the scion. Rubber bands are ideal for holding grafts because they expand with the growth of the scion and need not be removed because they rot away soon after growth begins. They must never be too tight, however, or they will injure the scions.

Cleft and side grafts are generally fastened with one or two opuntia spines or toothpicks run through the union to prevent slipping, and a wrapping of soft raffia or twine to prevent loosening. The wrapping and toothpicks should be removed after the graft has taken, but the opuntia spines may remain without danger if they are trimmed down to the stock. Firm, young spines from *O. subulata* are especially good for large grafts, while those from *O. ramosissima* are best for slender ones. Unlike toothpicks, which leave a scar when removed, or metal pins, which invariably lead to rot, opuntia spines are absorbed into the plant without a trace. Only one or two of these spines are needed to hold a stab graft in place.

Once the union is made and secured, no other treatment is necessary. Succulent grafts do not need to be protected with grafting wax or compounds, glass bottles or special shading, except that plants grafted out of doors should be covered with a paper sack for a few days until the graft is set. It is a good idea to examine the plants a few hours after grafting to make sure the rubber bands are not too tight and that the scions are still in place. Newly grafted plants should never be sprinkled overhead, as the cut surfaces may hold water, which will lead to rot and necessitate regrafting immediately. With any kind of luck at all and simple good treatment, succulent grafts should "take" and be growing in a few weeks.

CHAPTER EIGHT

Maintenance

No matter how succulents are propagated or where they are grown, they must have adequate care. The apartment dweller in New York with one plant and the collector in California with a thousand are faced with the same everyday chores of shading, watering, and feeding. Maintenance, more than anything else, spells the difference between success and failure with succulents.

Water

It may seem strange that the first and most important requirement of these drought-resistant plants is water. Yet without water at the right time and in the right quantities no succulent can live. Many succulents are ninety-five per cent water by weight, water patiently absorbed by deep-searching roots, water quickly guzzled in showers. And while they can store this moisture and keep most of it from evaporating, they must nevertheless drink deeply and well from time to time.

Watering is one of the greatest problems of the beginner because he falls into either one or another of these errors: he waters his succulents just as his other house plants or, knowing they are drought-resistant, he fails to water them at all. Both extremes lead to loss of roots and death of the plants. Watering succulents requires some know-how and an understanding of how these plants were meant to live and grow.

As a rule cultivated plants require more water because their root systems are smaller and dry out more quickly, especially when grown in pots. They seem to grow best when watered heavily at infrequent intervals. This allows the soil to dry to a medium point, and then the heavy application of water pushes out the carbon dioxide accumulated in the soil, and as the water drains away, new air circulates into the soil from above. By this means also roots grow throughout the entire soil mass and an occasional drying of the upper crust causes no damage. Frequent shallow waterings or constant saturation have the reverse effect on root growth and do not favor proper aeration of the soil.

It is almost impossible to tell how often any given succulent must be watered, for that depends entirely on the nature of the plant's root system, its age, location, and the season of the year. Of course newly set plants must not be watered for several days, and then very sparingly for a month or two. But established plants making fresh growth in spring or summer can be watered as often as the soil dries out. This is easily determined by scratching the surface of the soil a half inch deep with a matchstick or pencil. If the soil appears dry at that depth, the plant should be watered thoroughly.

The best time to water succulents is early in the morning, so that the plants and soil will be somewhat dried before evening. Opening a window or ventilator indoors after watering is a good practice, as succulents sometimes rot when they are bedded down for the night while still wet. It is always better to water succulents by irrigation rather than sprinkling. Indiscriminate watering overhead not only spoils the appearance of many plants that have a hairy or powdery surface, but constant wetting of stems and foliage may lead to rot. This does not mean, however, that an occasional spraying of the plants with water is not beneficial in keeping them clean and free of pests. But it must not be done too often, for the plants will rot if it is done in cool weather or late in the day, or burn if it is done in bright sunlight and great heat. Rain water is ideal for this purpose because it does not leave a chalky deposit to disfigure the plants, as does hard water. Whatever water is used for irrigation or spraying should be reasonably close to room or air temperature.

While succulents may be watered rather freely during their growing period in spring or summer, they require far less water as the weather becomes cooler in fall and winter. In this season most succulents begin their long period of hibernation, or rest, living largely from the moisture stored in their tissues. They should be watered only enough to keep them from shriveling. If the weather is cool and moist, young plants may safely go a week or two without water, older plants for a month or two. In outdoor growing areas winter rains alone will probably provide all the moisture needed. This dry rest hardens the plants against cold and rot, and is of utmost importance in succulent culture. As the weather begins to grow warm again in spring and the plants begin to take on a fresher, livelier appearance, water should be gradually increased to stimulate summer growth and bloom.

The technique of watering succulents is not a matter of formulas or schedules, but one which calls for much common sense and careful observation. There is only one reliable rule of thumb that can be recommended. Always water succulents thoroughly when they are growing, sparingly when they are resting, and not at all when you are in doubt.

Rest

Closely related to watering and all other phases of succulent culture is the vital need of succulents for rest. Nothing is so essential to their health and well-being, nothing is so much a part of their natural rhythm and way of life. Just as we sleep to regain our strength through the long, cold hours of the night, so these plants, exhausted from making new growth and flowers in spring and bearing fruit and seeds in summer, rest through the long, cold months of fall and winter. And as our body's needs and processes are less in sleep, so it is with these resting plants. They want neither much food nor water, coddling nor disturbance—only rest. This is true of all succulents. But it must be remembered that these seasons are reversed for some South African species. They grow in fall and winter and rest in spring and summer.

It is fairly easy to see when succulents are asleep and when they are awake. And there is nothing to be gained from forcing them unnaturally in either period. The results will always be the same—abnormal growth, loss of blooms, and greater susceptibility to cold and rot. Succulents should be allowed to rest easily and naturally for several months each year, for they are essentially slow-living, slow-growing plants. Their active season is rarely more than three or four months, and it is a serious mistake to treat them otherwise.

Cold and Shelter

Succulents that have been properly hardened by rest and reduced watering in fall and winter can withstand a remarkable amount of cold. It is not always low temperatures that damage these plants, but the combination of wet soil and soft, swollen stems and leaves that makes the first freeze so deadly. In their native habitat many succulents can take winter snow and freezing temperatures without damage because they have become hard and dry in the long resting period. But in cultivation these same plants are easily destroyed by even the lightest frost.

In Chapters Three and Four we have tried to indicate the

relative hardiness of various genera and species, but these estimates are hardly exact because so much depends on the age, location, soil, moisture, and condition of the plants. Of course no collector wishes to risk his plants unnecessarily, and it is a simple matter to winter most succulents safely.

In relatively frost-free outdoor growing areas succulents may usually be wintered with no protection at all if careful attention is given to proper hardening of the plants in fall. But if a hard freeze is predicted, a few tender plants in the ground may be protected by placing over them paper sacks large enough to clear the plants, as it is the free air space inside that does the job. Extensive outdoor plantings are usually protected with orchard burners which heat and circulate the air over the entire area.

In colder climates succulents must be wintered indoors in dry, well-lighted rooms, sun porches, verandas, or cellars, preferably at a constant temperature of 40 to 50°F. They should not be kept in highly heated rooms for long as this may force premature growth and greatly weaken the plants. Actually the ideal way to grow succulents in cold-winter areas is under glass. Any type of glasshouse will do provided it is sunny, dry, well ventilated, and kept at the optimum winter temperature of 40 to 50°F. The plants may be grown either in pots, on benches or, better still, in large raised beds on the floor. Occasionally cold or heated frames are used for wintering succulents, but the close atmosphere in these boxes is difficult to control and the plants may suffer from lack of ventilation.

Air, Light, and Shade

As much as water, rest, or heat, succulents need air, not only in the soil around their roots but all about them. They must never be grown in stuffy, poorly ventilated rooms or greenhouses, for they are by nature native to open places. Plants indoors should be aired at every opportunity, and windows or ventilators opened whenever the outside temperature is equal to or higher than the room temperature. By this means cold drafts are naturally avoided.

Even more important to the health and well-being of succulents is light. Indoors or out most species need a bright, sunny spot throughout the day to insure good growth and blooming. Potted specimens should be turned occasionally so that the light reaches all parts of the plant evenly, but plants in bud should not be moved or turned as the change in light may cause the buds to drop.

Whenever weather permits, succulents should be put out of doors to get the benefits of full daylight without the obstruction of glass. But they should not be put in full sunlight at once. Many species are burned by too much sun. Indoors they may be shaded lightly by curtains, venetian blinds, or shades; out of doors they can be put in the filtered shade under trees or covered with an improvised screen of lath, bamboo, or cloth. Large collections of shade-loving succulents, such as epiphyllums, are generally kept in cloth or lath houses, especially in their summer-blooming and growing period. But it is better to think of even these tree-dwelling succulents as plants for half sun rather than half shade. All succulents, even the so-called shade lovers, must have as much of the available sunlight in all seasons as they can possibly take without injury.

Food

Contrary to common belief, the soil in which succulents grow naturally is very rich. There is sand in the desert, to be sure, but with every torrential rain topsoil is washed down from the mountains and added to it; and a new crop of annual grasses and flowers springs up, matures, and dies to become rich leaf mold. The mineral content of this soil is very high

MAINTENANCE

Good lighting, ventilation, and cleanliness are the secrets of successful succulent culture under glass. In pots or in beds succulents make exciting greenhouse plants. The potted collection above features a wonderful group of Old Man Cacti at the center.

too, for the scant rainfall cannot wash these elements away. That is why we do not grow succulents in "pure" sand, why we are so careful to add rich topsoil, leaf mold, charcoal, and even lime to our mixtures.

But while succulent soils are rich in natural fertility they seldom receive much in the way of animal fertilizers. An occasional dead animal in the desert or the droppings of birds in jungle trees are about the limit of added fertilizers. In cultivation too succulents do not require much more than a well-balanced soil mixture in which to thrive. Bone meal is perhaps the only safe fertilizer for them, and should be added to the soil at the rate of one teaspoonful to each six-inch pot, or four pounds for each hundred square feet of planting area.

Occasionally tree-dwelling succulents such as epiphyllums and zygocacti are greatly benefited by a foliage spray of liquid fertilizer made by soaking one pound of cottonseed meal in five gallons of water for twenty-four hours. The clear liquid at the top is strained and sprayed on the plants two or three times during the growing season on cool or cloudy days. This very nearly duplicates the way they are fertilized in nature, as rain washes dust, decayed matter, and bird droppings from the higher leaves and branches of the trees down on their flat stems and aerial roots.

Actually the very best way to feed any succulent is by giving it new soil. Potted succulents should be taken from their pots and repotted in fresh soil whenever they become very root-bound, whenever they look weak or refuse to grow properly, or whenever pests or diseases are suspected at the roots. Most succulents will normally require repotting once every two years. Permanent outdoor plantings, however, are only occasionally fed with a light mulch of one part bone meal to thirty parts well-rotted leaf mold.

Pruning and Weeding

The need for pruning and weeding is not stressed often enough in succulent culture. All dead, diseased, or spindly leaves and branches should be removed from succulents, not only to improve their appearance but to admit light and air to the base or center of the plants. All cuts should be made with a sharp knife, clipper, or saw, preferably at a joint, and wounds over an inch in diameter dusted with powdered sulfur or charcoal to prevent infection. Very often drastic cutting of the upper part of stems, as when scions are taken for grafting, forces the remaining portion to make numerous branches, or offsets, at the cut. These may be allowed to grow on, or may be removed and rooted to make new plants.

Care should always be taken in cutting succulent flowers or seed pods to leave a small portion of the stem still attached to the plant. This stub will dry and drop off naturally without injuring the plant, but flowers or seeds torn or broken from the plant invariably cause injury or rot. It is imperative that the flower stalks of certain of the larger echeverias and aeoniums be removed before they bloom, because the plants die after blooming and generally leave no offsets. If the bloom stalks of aeoniums such as *A. tabulaeforme* are gouged out with a sharp knife from the center of the plant just before they elongate, the plant will not only remain but produce innumerable offsets around the cut. Flower stalks of the larger echeverias such as *E. gibbiflora* are allowed to develop to the bud stage, however, and then they are removed and treated like stem cuttings. Numerous plantlets form along these rooted flower stems and may be removed and grown on separately.

Another very important chore in growing succulents out of doors is the never ending battle against weeds. Nothing looks more forlorn, nothing harbors more danger from pests and diseases than a succulent bed overrun by weeds. Weeding must be done regularly and thoroughly with small tools and stout gloves, as weed killers and cultivators are impossible to use among these plants. Keeping the garden area generally free of weeds helps, regular edging of lawns and paths helps too, but when all is said and done it's a job for a gardener with a strong back, nimble fingers, and a patient soul.

Labels and Cataloguing

The final task in maintaining succulents properly is to keep them labeled. There are many kinds of labels in use, but a really satisfactory plant label must be small, inconspicuous, and reasonably lasting. Wood labels are cheap but they rot quickly; metal labels are durable but expensive. The very best kind for succulents are the thin, hard, plastic pot labels orchid growers use. They measure one half by three inches, and can be had in white and several soft colors. Names, dates, and descriptions written on them with an ordinary soft lead pencil will last for five years or more in the open, and they may be easily erased with a rubber eraser and the labels used again.

The really serious collector will also want to keep a small catalogue or notebook of his plants. Here the source and date of purchase or propagation of each plant are listed, the date of potting and repotting, and notes on blooming and seeding. Personal observations and experiments in watering or feeding are also recorded, and the resting period for various plants. Such a book is often more valuable than a dozen printed texts because it is personal and specific. It is not only the factual record of a collection of plants, but the story of the beginnings and growth of a valuable hobby.

CHAPTER NINE

Pests and Diseases

There are a number of pests and diseases that attack succulents, but all of them are easily recognized and controlled by simple methods. The best method, of course, is prevention. The collector who buys only healthy, vigorous stock; plants and spaces his collection carefully; and provides constant cleanliness, light, and air will rarely encounter more than two or three of these troubles in his career. For, like human ills, these disorders are not natural to succulents but the result of carelessness and poor growing conditions. It is far easier to keep these plants healthy by sound cultural practices than to cure them after they have become susceptible to pests and diseases through neglect and mistreatment.

Sucking Pests

The most insidious pests that attack succulents are those that suck the vital juices from stems and leaves and flowers. They are, as a rule, small and difficult to detect, and especially dangerous indoors, where they can multiply unchecked by their natural enemies. Hidden in the soil, in the crevices of roots and stems, in leaf joints and flower buds, they sap the plants of vitality, discolor leaves and flowers, and deform new growth and buds. Every new plant should be carefully checked for their presence, every old one examined when cleaning or repotting.

Perhaps the prime cause for the growth and spread of several of these pests are ants. They actually carry aphids and mealy bugs from one plant to another, put them to graze and nurse them, and in return eat the honeydew secretion which these pests produce. Controlling ants in the garden and greenhouse can markedly reduce the numbers and spread of these sucking pests. A good ant paste or powder should be used regularly on ant trails and nests, but never applied directly to the plants themselves.

The commonest sucking pest found on succulents are aphids or plant lice. These are small, soft-bodied, usually greenish insects which feed by thrusting their sharp beaks into tender young plant cells and sucking out the sap. The results are shown in discolored areas on the foliage, curling of leaves, and blighting of buds and fruit. Fortunately they are easily controlled by spraying with a forty per cent nicotine sulfate-soap solution made of one quart lukewarm water, one teaspoon mild soap flakes, and one half teaspoon Black Leaf 40. The plants should be watered thoroughly the day before spraying, shaded lightly after spraying, and the residue washed off in a few hours.

Certainly the most dangerous of all the sucking pests afflicting succulents are mealy bugs. These are fuzzy, gray or white, waxlike bodies about the size of a grain of wheat which are found on the spines, stems, or roots of succulent plants, especially when they are abnormally dry. Like aphids, they devitalize the plants by sucking cell juices; but, unlike them, the waxy-coated mealy bugs are far more difficult to kill. A few may be picked off plants with tweezers, killed by touching them with a camel's-hair brush dipped in denatured alcohol, or scrubbed off with a toothbrush dipped in the nicotine-soap solution, but extensive infestations can be removed only by more drastic measures. Large plants heavily infested aboveground can be hosed off thoroughly with a strong spray of water, which will not only knock off the bugs but wash away the sticky honeydew. Plants whose roots are infested may either be set with their pots in a pan of the nicotine solution to soak for thirty minutes or, if growing in the ground, a trench can be made around them and the soil thoroughly saturated with the same solution. If there is still any doubt that mealy bugs are in the soil, the plant should be taken out of the soil, its roots scrubbed and soaked quickly in the nicotine solution, and repotted or planted in fresh soil.

The most stubborn sucking pests affecting succulents are scale. They generally appear as brown or whitish raised spots about the size of pinheads on the stems, especially around the areoles of cacti. They are even more difficult to eradicate than mealy bugs because they are closely fitted with a strong shell-like covering that most sprays cannot penetrate. In mild infestations the affected parts may be scrubbed clean with a toothbrush dipped in nicotine-soap solution, but more serious attacks must be sprayed thoroughly at regular intervals with an oil-emulsion spray such as Volck according to the manufacturer's directions.

A very serious pest of some succulents is the root-knot nematode. It is a microscopic wormlike animal which enters the roots of plants such as echeverias and euphorbias and causes irregular swellings, or galls, which prevent the roots functioning properly. Affected plants are usually pale in color and somewhat dwarfed by this injury. Whenever suspicious swellings are found on the roots of any succulent, they should be root-pruned severely, dried out for a few days, and planted again in fresh soil. Since these pests are soil-borne, the old soil should be destroyed and the new soil used in the planting mixture sterilized if there is any doubt. This is easily done by heating the soil in an oven at 180°F. for an hour.

When succulents are kept too dry and warm, especially indoors in winter, thrips and red spiders may sometimes attack the plants, draining juices and leaving behind small yellow or white spots on the stems or leaves. These tiny mites, which look like bits of animated dust, are easily killed by washing the plants with a strong spray of water or, better still, by a thorough spraying with the usual nicotine-soap solution.

Chewing Pests

Nothing is so discouraging as to awake one morning to find one's pet echeveria riddled with snail holes or a choice mimicry plant pecked away by a bird. While these chewing pests are neither so insidious nor so deadly as the sucking ones, their kind of damage is just as exasperating. Fortunately, most of them can be dealt with promptly and easily.

Snails and slugs head the list as the chief spoilers of succulents. They are neither daunted by spiny plants nor beautiful blossoms, for they glide over one to eat the other with the greatest of ease. Every gardener should keep his grounds clear of all weeds and debris that might harbor these pests, and regularly set out prepared poison-bran baits that contain the attractant metaldehyde.

Beetles and sow bugs also occasionally attack succulents, eating at the base of mature plants and destroying seedlings outright. They should be stopped with the same bait used for snails and slugs.

Birds cannot really be blamed for finding some of the stone-mimicry mesembryanthemums delectable, for even the natives in South Africa relish their fresh acid taste. But nothing can so quickly reduce a fine collection of these plants to shambles as a thirsty bird. Outdoor plantings should be protected with a removable screen of wire mesh.

PESTS AND DISEASES

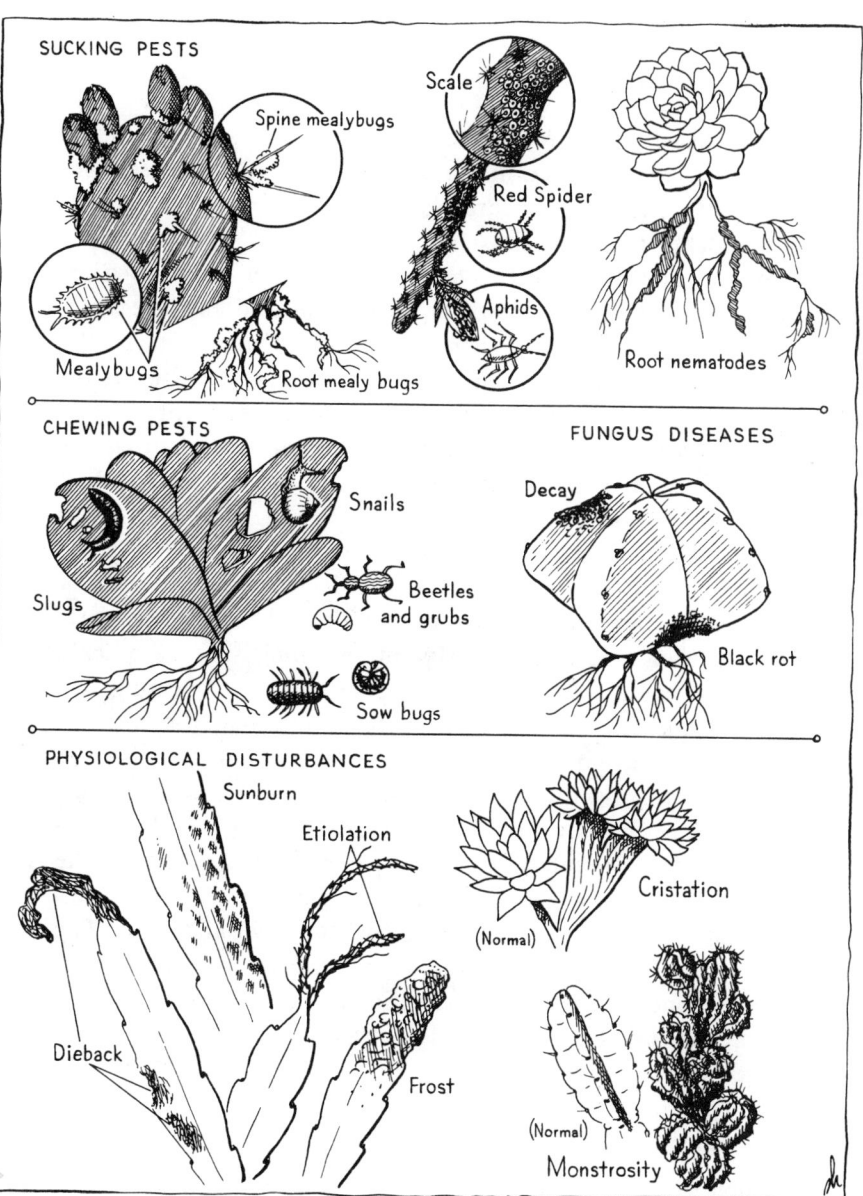

PESTS AND DISEASES

Fungus Diseases

While insect pests are of external origin and can invade even the best-kept collections unnoticed, fungus diseases are brought on entirely by carelessness and poor growing conditions. They can and must be prevented, for they are both needless and dangerous. Overwatering, underwatering, drips, bruises, broken roots, and improperly healed cuts are but a few of the ways in which decay begins. Once it starts, the plants take on a wilted, discolored appearance and refuse to grow. The soft decay spots must be found and cut back to sound tissue immediately, dusted with sulfur, and dried out thoroughly. It is important to use a sterile knife for the final cut in each case, as the decay organisms are easily transferred on hands and tools from one part to another.

Occasionally a type of black rot develops in the base of succulents through a break in the skin. The affected parts turn into a soft, black, mushy mass which spreads quickly into the center of the plant. A good tool for cleaning this type of infection is a sharpened teaspoon, which can scoop out the rotted portion quickly and neatly. The sound tissue should then be dusted with sulfur and allowed to callus slowly in a cool, dry place.

There are a number of lesser types of rot, ranging from the hard black spot which appears on cereus stems to the damping off of seedlings which are grown too wet and close. The first is treated by surgery and sulfur, the second by spraying the seed bed with Semesan. But in the last analysis these ailments are not so much specific diseases as symptoms of gross carelessness and neglect.

Physiological Disturbances

When succulents are suffering from mistreatment they often display it in other ways too. Plants that are getting too much

PESTS AND DISEASES

sun turn yellow or white on the top and south side, and eventually develop brown barklike scabs. Frosted plants become soft and mushy, and must be thawed gradually in the shade. Then their frozen parts can be cut away and the remaining plant dried and started again. Plants whose feeder roots have been damaged or starved wither, turn yellow, and die back. Lack of light and air causes succulents to make long. abnormal, snaky growths, a process called etiolation. All these ills are easily prevented by simply supplying the missing elements of good culture in each case.

A much subtler response in succulents, however, is the formation of crests and monstrosities. The cristate plant differs from the normal because its growing tip, instead of continuing its usual symmetrical form, develops laterally, producing a flattened growth like a cockscomb which may in time become twisted and convoluted. A monstrose plant, on the other hand, develops multiple centers at its growing tip from which irregular growths spring.

No one knows exactly why so many succulents develop these strange deformities. Some believe it is caused by mechanical damage to the growing tip or disease, overnourishment or undernourishment, heredity or environment. The battle rages on. But in the meanwhile collectors have made capital of this curious physiological response and made collecting these freakish plants a full-time hobby in itself.

The Human Element

The last and perhaps the most serious threat affecting the health and happiness of succulents is the people who grow them. There is no pest or disease so deadly as the ignorant or overzealous gardener who depends on fertilizers, miracle drugs, and gimmicks to cover up and cure the results of his hasty planting and chronic neglect. Perhaps it is human nature to seek easy palliatives to hide our own deliberate failings. But

Many collectors are fascinated by the relatively common occurrence of deformed or fasciated growths in succulents. These crests and monstrosities are often curiously beautiful and are usually perpetuated by grafting.

PESTS AND DISEASES

PESTS AND DISEASES

succulents properly located, carefully planted, sensibly watered, and thoroughly rested need little or no fertilizers, hormones, etc. The excessive use of these stimulants denotes one of two things: either the plants have been grown improperly to start with, or they are being forced beyond their normal growth and bloom because of the grower's impatience.

A healthy plant making normal growth and bloom needs no further stimulation, even as you and I do not take drugs unless we definitely need them. But there are unfortunately gardening hypochondriacs as well as medical hypochondriacs who insist on dosing and spraying their plants regularly, whether they need it or not. It is a vicious habit, aided and abetted by the patent-cure peddlers, two-bit experts, and the grower's own irresistible impulse to play doctor. Don't feed your plants unless they show they are hungry. Don't water them unless they are thirsty. Don't medicate them unless they are obviously ill. In short, learn how your succulents were meant to grow in nature and try to give them those conditions as nearly as you can. Then stop playing God! Sit back and enjoy your plants, for you cannot really *grow* succulents —they grow by themselves.

CHAPTER TEN

Books about Succulents

One of the best ways to learn more about succulents is to read some of the many fine books that have been written on them recently. Not so many years ago the collector seeking books on succulents could find relatively few. Most of the serious works in the field were ponderous German tomes of little interest to the beginner. But in recent years the problem has reversed itself completely. There are so many books on cacti and other succulents in English now that the beginner is at a loss to know which ones to choose. Some of these books are cheap, popular treatments hardly worth reading; others are serious scientific monographs so difficult that the beginner cannot hope to understand them. So it is important to set down here a few books that every amateur will find both valuable and interesting, books that have stood out from the welter of titles as being both readable and authoritative.

A really different book for the beginning collector as well as the advanced hobbyist is *Cacti and Succulents for the Amateur* by Charles Glass and Robert Foster (Abbey Garden Press, Santa Barbara, 1976). Many of the newer and more unusual kinds of cacti and other succulents are pictured and described in family groups.

To better understand the meaning and pronunciation of the

scientific terms and plant names he will find in his reading, every amateur should have the *Glossary of Succulent Plant Terms* by W. Taylor Marshall and R. S. Woods (Abbey Garden Press, 1945). It is a wonderfully useful book, and though long out-of-print, it is once again available in a special Xerox series from Abbey Garden Press.

Of books on cacti the outstanding work is certainly the monumental four-volume *The Cactaceae*, by N. L. Britton and J. N. Rose. It is a long and difficult work, however, and now very much out of date. Even in the edition reprinted by Dover Publications (New York, 1963) it is fairly expensive. But there is one modern up-to-date book on the Cactus family that is a "must" for every student of cacti. It is *Cactus Lexicon* by Curt Backeberg (Blandford Press, Poole, England, 1977). Here in one volume, profusely illustrated with hundreds of photographs, the entire Cactus family is surveyed and the Britton and Rose classification brought up to date in the light of recent discoveries. Another useful handbook is *Cacti* by J. Borg (Blandford Press, Poole, England, Fourth edition, 1970).

For the reader interested in a closer study of the other succulents there is one indispensable handbook, *Lexicon of Succulent Plants* by Hermann Jacobsen (Blandford Press, Poole, England, 1977). It describes in alphabetical order for easy reference the habitat and forms of over a thousand species.

There are many colorful picture books of cacti and other succulents, but one of the finest is *The Illustrated Encyclopedia of Succulents* by Gordon Rowley (Crown Publishers, New York, 1978). Over 250 species are shown in brilliant color to illustrate a fine general treatment of succulent plants the world over. Also valuable as a picture reference is *The Illustrated Reference on Cacti and Other Succulents* in five volumes by Edgar and Brian Lamb (Blandford

Press, Poole, England, 1955-1978).

For the collector who wishes to specialize in particular families of succulents we might recommend the following: *The Aloes of South Africa* by Gilbert Westacott Reynolds (A. A. Balkema, Rotterdam, Fourth edition, 1982) and his *The Aloes of Tropical Africa and Madagascar* (The Aloes Book Fund, Mbabane, Swaziland, 1966); *Agaves of Continental North America* by Howard Scott Gentry (Univ. of Arizona Press, Tucson, 1982); *Echeveria* by Eric Walther (California Academy of Sciences, San Francisco, 1972); *Haworthia and Astroloba* by John Pilbeam (Timber Press, Portland, Oregon, 1983) and his *Mammillaria* (B. T. Batsford, London, 1981).

There are many more of these specialized studies of particular succulents ranging from slight pamphlets to weighty monographs. They appear and disappear constantly. The interested reader should avail himself of the excellent annotated catalogs of these books published annually by Abbey Garden Press, P. O. Box 3010, Santa Barbara, CA 93130.

And, finally, to keep up with current developments in the cactus and succulent world every enthusiast should subscribe to the *Cactus and Succulent Journal*. It is published bimonthly by The Cactus and Succulent Society of America, P. O. Box 3010, Santa Barbara, CA 93130, and is included with membership in the Society.

Index

Adromischus, 67, 68
   clavifolius, 67
   cooperi, 67
   cristatus, 67
   maculatus, 67
Aeonium, 84–85
   arboreum, 84
   arboreum var. atropurpureum, 84
   caespitosum, 84
   canariense, 85
   decorum, 84
   haworthii, 84
   nobile, 85, 86
   tabulaeforme, 85, 86, 212
Aeroplane Propellers, 69
African Living Rock, 114
Agave, 13, 64–66, 95, 196
   americana, 64
   americana var. marginata, 64
   americana var. medio-picta, 64
   americana var. striata, 64
   attenuata, 64–66
   filifera, 66
   stricta, 66
   victoriae-reginae, 66
Agave Cactus, 48
Air Plant, 78

Aloe, 7, 13, 95–98, 196
   africana, 97, 98
   arborescens, 97
   aristata, 96
   brevifolia, 96
   ciliaris, 97
   ferox, 97
   globosa, 96
   marlothii, 97
   mitriformis, 97
   nobilis, 97
   perryi, 96
   striata, 97
   variegata, 96, 98
   vera, 96
Amaryllis family, 64–66
Amethyst Plant, 82
Anacampseros, 130–31
   alstonii, 130
   lanceolata, 130
   papyracea, 130
   telephiastrum, 130
   tomentosa, 130
Ants, 216
Aphids, 216
Apicra, 102–3
   pentagona, 103

INDEX

Aporocactus flagelliformis, 42
Areole, 26, 54, 90
Argyroderma, 116
  braunsii, 116
  octophyllum, 116
  roseum, 116
Ariocarpus fissuratus, 47
Arizona Organ Pipe, 39
Arrangements, 154–57
Astrophytum, 51, 173
  asterias, 51
  capricorne, 51
  myriostigma, 51
  ornatum, 51
Aztekium ritteri, 48

Brain Cacti, 48
Bryophyllum, 14, 76, 77–78, 196
  crenatum, 78
  daigremontianum, 78
  fedtschenkoi, 78
  pinnatum, 77
  scandens, 78
  tubiflorum, 78
  uniflorum, 78
Bulbine, 103
  alooides, 103
  caulescens, 103
Bunny Ears, 33
Burro's Tail, 81
Buying, 187–88
Byrnesia weinbergii, 82

Baby Toes, 117
Ball Cacti, 52
Barbados gooseberries, 30
Barrel Cacti, 48–51, 153, 173
Basket Ball Euphorbia, 92
Bearded Starfish Flower, 122
Beaucarnea, 183
Beaver Tail, 33
Beetles, 218
Bird's Nest Cactus, 56
Birds, 218
Bishop's Cap, 51
Bitter Aloes, 96
Black Starfish, 122
Blue Barrel, 50
Blue Chalk Sticks, 87
Blue Mitre, 38
Books, succulent, 2, 186, 227–29
Boston Bean, 81
Bowiea volubilis, 103–4
Boxing Gloves, 34

Cactus family, 2, 19, 23, 25–61, 198
  classification of, 28–29
  defined, 26
  distribution of, 26–27
  history, 27–29
  nomenclature, 28–29
Callusing, 196
Candelabra Cacti, 36–38
Candle Plant, 86
Candy Stick, 87
Caralluma, 122
  burchardii, 122
  europaea, 122
  lutea, 122
Carnegiea gigantea, 36
Carpobrotus, 108
  acinaciformis, 108
  chilensis, 108
  edulis, 108
Carrion Flowers, 120
Cataloguing, 213

INDEX

Century Plant, 2, 64, 66, 95, 153
Cephalium, 54
Cephalocereus, 39
  chrysacanthus, 39
  senilis, 39, 43
Cephalophyllum, 108-9
  alstonii, 109
  spongiosum, 109
  tricolorum, 109
Cereus, 36, 47
  dayamii, 36
  jamacaru, 36
  peruvianus, 36, 198
  peruvianus var. *monstrosus*, 93
Cereus tribe, 35
Ceropegia, 125-27
  barklyi, 127
  debilis, 127
  dichotoma, 126
  fusca, 126
  radicans, 127
  sandersonii, 126
  stapeliiformis, 126
  woodii, 126
Ceropegia tribe, 125-27
Chain Plant, 131
Chalk Lettuce, 74
Chamaecereus silvestrii, 46-47
Cheiridopsis, 112
  candidissima, 112
  cigarettifera, 112
  meyeri, 112
  peculiaris, 112
  pillansii, 112
Chenille Plant, 73
Chin Cacti, 51-52
Chinese Lanterns, 78
Cholla, 32-34
Christmas Cactus, 60
Christmas Cheer, 81

Cissus, 128
  cactiformis, 128
  quadrangularis, 128
Cleistocactus, 40-41
  baumannii, 40
  hyalacanthus, 41
  strausii, 40
Climbing Cacti, 41-42, 57, 183
Cob Cacti, 46
Cobweb Houseleek, 83
Cockscomb Sedum, 80
Cold, 206-7
Collecting, 1, 24, 185-87
Common Houseleek, 84
Cone Plants, 115
Conophytum, 115-16
  braunsii, 116
  giftbergensis, 116
  meyerae, 116
  minutum, 116
Containers, 135-40, 149, 153
Coral Aloe, 97
Corn Cob Euphorbia, 92
Corsages, 157-58
Coryphantha, 54-55, 56
  bumamma, 56
  clava, 56
  elephantidens, 56
  erecta, 56
  macromeris, 56
  radians, 56
Cotyledon, 67-68
  ausana, 68
  cacalioides, 68
  orbiculata, 68
  teretifolia, 68
  undulata, 68
Cotyledon tribe, 67-68
Cow's Horns, 93
Crab Cactus, 61

233

INDEX

Crassula, 69–70, 183
 arborescens, 69
 argentea, 69
 barbata, 70
 deltoidea, 70
 falcata, 69
 hemisphaerica, 70
 justi-corderoyi, 70
 lactea, 70
 lycopodioides, 70
 multicava, 70
 perforata, 69
 pyramidalis, 70
 teres, 70
 tetragona, 69
 triebneri, 70
Crassula family, 66–86, 196
Crassula tribe, 68–72
Crimson Parodia, 52
Cristation, 221
Crocodile Aloe, 96
Crown Cacti, 46
Crown of Thorns, 88, 91
Cryophytum crystallinum, 107–8
Cuttings, 194–97
Cyanotis somaliensis, 131–32
Cylindropuntia, 32–34

Daisy family, 86–88
Dam's Chin, 52
Dasylirion, 183
Decay, 142, 220
Delosperma echinatum, 107
Desert Rose, 110
Deutsche Kaiserin, 60
Devil's Club, 92
Dicotyledons, 9, 26, 198
Disbudding, 212
Discocactus, 54

Diseases, 220–21
Dish gardens, 149–53
Dominoes, 33
Dragon's Blood Sedum, 80
Drainage, 140, 143–49, 162
Drosanthemum, 107
 floribundum, 107
 speciosum, 107
Dudleya, 14, 74
 brittonii, 74
 candida, 74
 farinosa, 74
 ingens, 74
 pulverulenta, 74
Dumpling Cactus, 48
Dwarf Chin, 52
Dyckia, 183

Eagle Claw Cactus, 50
Easter Cactus, 61
Easter Lily Cacti, 44
Echeveria, 72–74, 82, 154, 157, 173, 217
 amoena, 73, 76
 carnicolor, 73
 crenulata, 74
 derenbergii, 73
 elegans, 73
 expatriata, 73
 gibbiflora, 73, 76, 196, 212
 gibbiflora var. *carunculata*, 74
 gibbiflora var. *crispata*, 74
 gibbiflora var. *metallica*, 73
 glauca, 73
 harmsii, 73
 hoveyi, 74
 leucotricha, 73
 microcalyx, 73
 peacockii, 73

INDEX

Echeveria: (cont.)
  pulvinata, 73
  secunda, 73
  setosa, 73
  weinbergii, 82
Echeveria tribe, 72–76
Echidnopsis cereiformis, 124
Echinocactus, 50
  grusonii, 50
  horizonthalonius, 50
  ingens, 50
Echinocereus, 43–44
  dasyacanthus, 43
  delaetii, 43
  pentalophus, 43
  reichenbachii, 43
  rigidissimus, 43
Echinofossulocactus, 48
Echinopsis, 44, 139, 173
  calochlora, 44
  campylacantha, 44
  eyriesii, 44
  huottii, 44
  multiplex, 44
  obrepanda, 44
  oxygona, 44
  rhodotricha var. *argentinensis,* 44
  silvestrii, 44
Elephant Bush, 131
Elephant Grass, 70
Elk's Horn Euphorbia, 93
Elk's Horns, 110
Empress of Germany, 60
Encephalocarpus strobiliformis, 47–48
Epiphyllum, 14, 41, 57–60, 139, 157, 179, 183, 198, 208, 211
  anguliger, 57
  crenatum, 58
  hybrids: Ballerina 60, Bambi

Epiphyllum, hybrids: *(cont.)*
  60, Conway's Giant 58, Eden 58, Friedrich Werner-Beul 58, Gloria 58, Hermosissimus 58, Latona 58, Oriole 58, Padre 58, Peter Pan 60, Rosetta 58–60, Scarlet Giant 58, Sea Breeze 60, Sun Goddess 58, Vive Rouge 58
  latifrons, 57
  strictum, 57
Epiphytes, 35, 41, 57
Eriocereus, 41
  bonplandii, 41
  regelii, 41
Espaliers, 179–83
Espostoa lanata, 40
Etiolation, 221
Euphorbia, 88–94, 197, 217
  abyssinica, 93
  bergeri, 91
  bupleurifolia, 92
  canariensis, 93
  caput-medusae, 91, 94
  cereiformis, 90, 92, 94
  clandestina, 92
  coerulescens, 93
  dregeana, 88
  globosa, 91, 92
  grandicornis, 93
  hermentiana, 93
  heterophylla, 88
  horrida, 92
  inermis, 91
  lactea var. *cristata,* 93
  mammillaris, 90, 92, 94
  marginata, 88
  mauritanica, 88
  meloformis, 92, 94
  obesa, 91, 94
  opuntioides, 90

INDEX

Euphorbia: (cont.)
  polygona, 93
  pseudocactus, 92
  pulcherrima, 88
  splendens, 88, 91
  valida, 92
Euphorbia family, 88–94, 198

Faucaria, 110–12
  bosscheana, 112
  tigrina, 110
  tuberculosa, 112
Feather Cactus, 55
Fenestraria, 117
  aurantiaca, 117
  rhopalophylla, 117
Ferocactus, 50
  alamosanus, 50
  latispinus, 50
  nobilis, 50
  rectispinus, 50
  wislizenii, 50
Fertilizers, 140, 208–11
Firecracker Aloe, 97
Fishhook Barrel, 50
Frerea indica, 120
Frithia pulchra, 117
Frost, 206–7, 221

Gasteria, 14, 98–101
  acinacifolia, 101
  carinata, 101
  maculata, 100
  verrucosa, 100
Geranium family, 127–28
Ghost Plant, 82
Giant Starfish, 122

Giant-spined Barrel, 50
Gibbaeum, 117
  album, 117
  heathii, 117
  shandii, 117
Glochids, 32
Glottiphyllum, 109–10
  linguiforme, 110
Goat's Horn, 51
Gold-spined Aloe, 97
Golden Ball, 52
Golden Barrel, 50
Golden Easter Lily Cactus, 46
Golden Old Man, 39
Golden Sedum, 81
Golden Stars, 55
Grafting, 197–202
Grape family, 128
Graptopetalum, 82
  amethystinum, 82
  paraguayense, 82
  weinbergii, 82
Green Rosebuds, 85
Greenhouse, 207
Greenovia, 85
  aurea, 85
  dodrentalis, 85
Grizzly Bear Cactus, 33–34
Ground covers, 176–79
Gymnocalycium, 51–52
  damsii, 52
  fleischerianum, 52
  mihanovichii, 51–52
  quehlianum, 52
  schickendantzii, 52
  venturianum, 52

Hairy Starfish Flower, 122
Hanging baskets, 183–84

INDEX

Haworthia, 101–2, 153, 196
  cymbiformis, 102
  fasciata, 102
  margaritifera, 102
  reinwardtii, 102
  retusa, 102
  truncata, 102
  viscosa, 102
Hechtia, 183
Hedgehog Agave, 66
Hedgehog Cacti, 43–47
Heliocereus, 41, 58
  speciosus, 41
Hen and Chickens, 2, 73, 76
Hereroa, 110
  dyeri, 110
  nelii, 110
Hoodia, 124
  bainii, 124
  gordoni, 124
  macrantha, 124
Hottentot Fig, 108
House plants, 133–35
Houseleek, 83
Hoya carnosa, 119
Huernia, 122–24
  hystrix, 124
  keniensis, 124
  pillansii, 124
  primulina, 122
  schneideriana, 124
  zebrina, 124
Hylocereus undatus, 42
Hymenocyclus, 108
  croceus, 108
  herrei, 108
  purpureo-croceus, 108

Ice Plant, 107–8

Inchworm Plant, 86
Indian Comb Cactus, 38
Indian Head, 52

Jade Plant, 69
Jerusalem Thorn, 169
Jewel Plant, 117
Joseph's Coat, 33

Kalanchoe, 76–77
  beharensis, 77
  blossfeldiana, 77
  carnea, 77
  flammea, 77
  marmorata, 77
  tomentosa, 77
Kalanchoe tribe, 76–78
Karroo Rose, 116
Kitchingia, 76
  mandrakensis, 77
Kleinia, 86–87
  anteuphorbium, 86
  articulata, 86, 88
  ficoides, 87
  mandraliscae, 87
  neriifolia, 86
  pendula, 86
  radicans, 87
  repens, 87
  tomentosa, 87, 88
Knobby Tiger Jaws, 112

Labels, 213
Lace Aloe, 96
Lace Cactus, 43

INDEX

Lampranthus, 106
  aureus, 106
  brownii, 106
  coccineus, 106
  conspicuus, 106
  roseus, 106
  spectabilis, 106
  zeyheri, 106
Landscaping, 1, 33, 159–84
Lapidaria margaretae, 116–17
Lemaireocereus, 38–39
  marginatus, 38
  pruinosus, 38
  thurberi, 39
Lemon Ball, 52
Lemon Vine, 30
Leopard's Spots, 67
Leuchtenbergia principis, 48
Light, 19, 208
Lilac Easter Lily Cactus, 44
Lily family, 7, 94–104
Link Cactus, 61
Lithops, 14, 114–15
  aucampiae, 115
  bella, 115
  comptonii, 115
  fulleri, 115
  lesliei, 115
  pseudotruncatella, 115
Little Pickles, 87
Living Rock Cacti, 47–48
Lobivia, 44, 46, 47, 173
  aurea, 46
  backebergii, 46
  famatimensis, 46
  hertrichiana, 46
Lobster Claws, 112
Lophocereus, 39
  schottii, 39
  schottii var. *monstrosus,* 39

Lophophora williamsii, 48
Love Plant, 130

Madagascar Jasmine, 119
Maintenance, 23, 162, 203–13, 221–225
Mammillaria, 54–56, 153, 173
  bocasana, 55
  bombycina, 56
  camptotricha, 56
  candida, 56
  compressa, 56
  elongata, 55
  fragilis, 55
  hahniana, 56
  kewensis, 56
  parkinsonii, 56
  plumosa, 55
  spinosissima, 56
  vaupelii, 56
Mealy bugs, 142, 188, 216–17
Melocactus intortus, 54
Melon Cacti, 52–54
Mesembryanthemum family, 26, 104–19, 176, 183
Mexican Dwarf Tree, 34
Mexican Fire Plant, 88
Mexican Firecracker, 73
Mexican Giant Cactus, 38
Mexican Living Rock, 47
Mexican Old Man, 39, 43
Midget Pine Tree, 69
Milk Tree, 93
Milkweed family, 119–27, 198
Mistletoe Cactus, 61
Mitre Aloe, 97
Monocotyledons, 9
Monstrosities, 221

INDEX

Monvillea, 40
 cavendishii, 40
 spegazzinii, 40
Moonstones, 75
Mother of Hundreds, 56
Mulching, 143, 211
Myrtillocactus geometrizans, 38

Nematodes, 217
Night-blooming Cereus, 42, 57
Nolina, 183
Nopalxochia phyllanthoides, 60
Notocactus, 52
 apricus, 52
 leninghausii, 52
 ottonis, 52
 scopa, 52
 submammulosus, 52
Nyctocereus serpentinus, 40, 42, 198

Obregonia denegrii, 48
Old Lady Cactus, 56
Old Man of the Andes, 40
Old Man Cacti, 36, 39–40
Old Man Opuntia, 34
Ophthalmophyllum, 117–18
 friedrichiae, 118
 herrei, 118
 maughanii, 118
Opuntia, 32–34, 196
 basilaris, 33
 erectoclada, 33
 erinacea, 33
 erinacea var. *ursina,* 34
 fragilis, 169

Opuntia: (cont.)
 fragilis var. *tuberiformis,* 29
 glomerata, 34
 mammillata, 34
 microdasys, 33
 monacantha variegata, 33
 phaeacantha, 169
 ramosissima, 202
 rhodantha, 169
 strobiliformis, 34
 subulata, 198, 202
 vestita, 34
 vilis, 34
Orange Cob Cactus, 46
Orchid Cacti, 41, 58
Oreocereus celsianus, 40
Organ Pipe Cacti, 36, 38–39, 153
Oscularia, 106
 caulescens, 106
 deltoides, 106
 deltoides var. *muricata,* 106
Othonna crassifolia, 87
Owl's Eyes, 56
Ox Tongue, 100

Pachycereus, 36–38
 pecten-aboriginum, 38
 pringlei, 38
Pachyphytum, 75, 82
 bracteosum, 75, 82
 compactum, 75
 oviferum, 75
Pachyveria, 75
 clavifolia var. *cristata,* 75
 glauca, 75
 scheideckeri, 75
Painted Lady, 73
Panda Plant, 77

INDEX

Paper-spined Opuntia, 34, 51
Parkinsonia aculeata, 169
Parodia, 52
   aureispina, 52
   mutabilis, 52
   sanguiniflora, 52
Partridge-Breast Aloe, 97
Patterned bedding, 169–73
Peanut Cactus, 46–47
Pelargonium, 127–28
   echinatum, 127
   tetragonum, 128
Pen Wiper Plant, 77
Pereskia, 25–26, 30–32, 47
   aculeata, 30
   aculeata var. godseffiana, 30
Peruvian Old Man, 40
Peruvian Rock Cactus, 93
Peruvian Torch, 36
Pests, 215–18
Peyote, 48
Pincushion Cacti, 54–56
Pine Cone Cactus, 47–48
Pineapple Euphorbia, 92
Pink Chin, 52
Pink Easter Lily Cactus, 44
Pink Moon Cactus, 41
Plaid Cactus, 51
Planters, 183
Platyopuntia, 32–34, 198
Pleiospilos, 114
   bolusii, 114
   nelii, 114
   simulans, 114
Plover's Eggs, 67
Plush Plant, 73
Poinsettia, 88, 91
Porcupine Huernia, 124
Portulaca, 130
   grandiflora, 130
   oleracea, 130

Portulaca family, 26, 128–31
Portulacaria, 131
   afra, 131
   afra var. tricolor, 131
Potting, 140–43, 211
Powder Puff Cactus, 55
Pretty Pebbles, 67
Prickly Pear, 27, 32–34
Proliferations, 196
Propagation, 14, 188–202
Pruning, 212
Pseudorhipsalis macrantha, 61
Purslane, 130
Pussy Ears, 132
Puya, 183
Pyramid Crassula, 70

Queen of the Night, 42

Rainbow Bush, 131
Rainbow Cactus, 43
Rat-tail Cactus, 42
Rattlesnake Crassula, 70
Rebutia, 46
   kupperiana, 46
   minuscula, 46
   violaciflora, 46
Red Dragon Flower, 124
Red spider, 218
Rest, 205–6
Rhipsalis, 61, 198
   cereuscula, 61
   crispata, 61
   houlletiana, 61
   mesembryanthemoides, 61
   paradoxa, 61
Rice Cactus, 61

INDEX

Rochea, 70–72
   coccinea, 70
Rock gardens, 160–69
Rosary Vine, 126
Rose Moss, 130

Saguaro, 2, 36
St. Andrew's Cross, 70
Sand Dollar, 51
Scale, 142, 188, 217
Scarlet Bugler, 40
Scarlet Paint Brush, 69
Schlumbergera gaertneri, 61
Sea Fig, 108
Sea Shells, 67
Sedum, 14, 78–82, 157, 169, 173, 176, 183
   acre, 80
   adolphi, 81
   allantoides, 81
   amecamecanum, 81
   compressum, 81
   dasyphyllum, 80, 153
   guatemalense, 81
   moranense, 81
   morganianum, 81
   multiceps, 81
   pachyphyllum, 81
   palmeri, 81
   praealtum, 80–81
   reflexum var. *cristatum*, 80
   sexangulare, 80
   sieboldii, 80
   spathulifolium, 80
   spectabile, 80
   spurium var. *coccineum*, 80
   stahlii, 81
   treleasei, 81

Sedum tribe, 78–83
Seeds, 189–94
Selenicereus, 42, 58, 61
   grandiflorus, 42
   macdonaldiae, 42, 198
   pteranthus, 42
Sempervivum, 83–84, 169, 176
   arachnoideum, 83
   calcaratum, 84
   montanum, 83
   tectorum var. *calcareum*, 84
Sempervivum tribe, 83–86
Senecio, 87
   scaposus, 87
   stapeliiformis, 87
Shade, 19, 135, 169, 208
Shark's Head, 117
Shelter, 206–7
Shining Ball, 44
Shriner's Plant, 110
Silken Pincushion, 55–56
Silver Ball, 52
Silver Beads, 70
Silver Crown, 68
Silver Dollar, 70
Silver Torch, 40
Silverskins, 116
Slender Torch Cacti, 36, 40–41
Slugs, 218
Snails, 218
Snake Cactus, 40
Snake's Head Euphorbia, 91
Snow on the Mountain, 88
Snowball Pincushion, 56
Snowdrop Cactus, 61
Soil, 19, 118, 140–42, 192, 194, 208–11
Soldier, 92
Sow bugs, 218
Split Rock, 114
Staking, 143, 197

INDEX

Stapelia, 121–22, 153
  berlinensis, 122
  gettleffii, 122
  gigantea, 122, 125
  hirsuta, 122
  nobilis, 122
  pulvinata, 122
  variegata, 121, 125
  variegata var. *cristata*, 122
Stapelia tribe, 120–25
Star Cacti, 51
Starfish Flower, 121
Stenocactus multicostatus, 48
Stephanotis floribunda, 119
Stetsonia coryne, 38
Stone Faces, 115
Stone mimicry, 14, 47, 112–14
Stonecrop, 80
Stones, 153, 163
String of Buttons, 69
Strombocactus disciformis, 48
Succulents
  defined, 2, 6–8, 9, 19
  development of, 2–8, 9–15, 25 63, 132
  distribution of, 8–9, 19
Sun Cereus, 41
Sun Cup, 52
Sunburn, 220–21
Sweetheart Geranium, 128

Tephrocacti, 32, 34, 198
Terrariums, 153
Thimble Cactus, 55
Thrips, 218
Tiger Aloe, 97
Tiger Jaws, 110
Titanopsis calcarea, 117
Toad Cactus, 122

Tom Thumb Cactus, 52
Tongue Leaf, 110
Torch Cacti, 35–41
Totem Pole Cactus, 39
Tradescantia, 131
  fluminensis, 131
  navicularis, 131
Tree-dwelling Cacti, 8, 41, 57–61, 183
Trichocereus, 39, 44
  candicans, 39
  schickendantzii, 39
  spachianus, 39, 198
Trichodiadema densum, 110
Tricolor Jade Plant, 69
Turk's Cap Cactus, 27–28, 54

Urbinia, 75
  agavoides, 75
  corderoyi, 75
  purpusii, 75

Velvet Elephant Ear, 77
Ventilation, 204, 207–8
Victory Plant, 112

Wall Pepper, 80
Wall plantings, 173–76
Wandering Jew family, 131–32
Water, 9–13, 19–23, 143–49, 203–5
Wax Vine, 119
Waxy Tiger Jaws, 112
Weeding, 212–13
White Chin, 52
White Torch, 40–41

INDEX

White Torch Cactus, 39
Window boxes, 134–35
Windowed plants, 14, 101, 113, 117–18

Xerophytes, 6–8

Yucca, 7, 183

Zebra Flower, 124
Zebra Haworthia, 102
Zygocactus, 60–61, 157, 211
   truncatus, 60